Transforming Technical Services through Training and Development

Transforming Technical Services through Training and Development

Edited by Marlee Givens and Sofia Slutskaya

IN COLLABORATION WITH CORE PUBLISHING

CHICAGO | 2023

ISBN: 978-0-8389-4877-4 (paper)

Library of Congress Cataloging-in-Publication Data

Names: Givens, Marlee, 1970- editor. | Slutskaya, Sofia, 1967- editor. | Core: Leadership, Infrastructure, Futures (Organization)

Title: Transforming technical services through training and development / edited by Marlee Givens and Sofia Slutskaya in collaboration with Core Publishing.

Description: Chicago : ALA Editions, [2023]. | Includes bibliographical references and index. | Summary: "This book offers technical services managers and trainers useful examples for creating a learning culture in their departments. Readers will learn how to identify and create training opportunities and incorporate training into everyday workflows"—Provided by publisher.

Identifiers: LCCN 2022018815 | ISBN 9780838948774 (paperback)

Subjects: LCSH: Technical services (Libraries)—Employees—Training of—United States.

Classification: LCC Z688.6.U6 T735 2023 | DDC 023/.3—dc23/eng/20220628

LC record available at https://lccn.loc.gov/2022018815

Cover design by Alejandra Diaz. Text design by Kim Hudgins in the Skolar Latin, Source Sans, and Laski Slab typefaces.

⊚ This paper meets the requirements of ANSI/NISO Z39.48-1992 (Permanence of Paper).

Printed in the United States of America
27 26 25 24 23   5 4 3 2 1

Contents

Introduction

AT THE 2020 ALA VIRTUAL EVENT, THE EDITORS OF THIS BOOK INTRODUCED the idea of the technical services learning organization. They proposed that by borrowing methods and best practices from instructional design, lean management, and "training within industry" (TWI), libraries could develop a learning culture. By incorporating formal and informal staff development into the everyday work of their employees, libraries could achieve continuous improvement in service delivery.

The editors could not have anticipated the COVID-19 pandemic and the subsequent pivot to remote work and learning, which required the rapid development of new skills. However, they saw parallels with TWI, a program created by the U.S. Department of War as a response to the need for skilled workers during World War II. Between 1941 and 1945, 1.6 million people were trained in the production of war materials. The statistics collected by the program showed not only increased productivity and reduced training time, but also a significant reduction in grievances by workers. In addition to all the other positive results, training helps employees cope with stress and deal with uncertainty (Graupp and Wrona 2016, xxiv–xxvi).

TWI emphasizes training the trainer, and the TWI program produced a lot of documentation related to selecting potential trainers, teaching them, and providing job aids for them to use in organizing training. The editors had experience applying these methods in the technical services context, during a major cross-training project in 2017. Subject matter experts across several functional areas created standard work documentation, and then developed and delivered training based on the documentation. Training involved not just learning procedures, but also identifying experts and engaging in hands-on practice immediately following training, using the documentation. TWI considers the practice phase an opportunity to make improvements in the procedures and in subsequent training programs.

One of the key components of TWI is its approach to job instruction. In this approach, instructors learn to break down jobs into clearly defined steps. This is also one of the principles of instructional design. Breaking down job functions into discrete tasks and skills not only helps the trainer; it also helps the adult learner manage the cognitive load of learning something new. Before beginning the cross-training project, the editors and their colleagues invested time in identifying basic and advanced tasks and skills in each functional area of technical services. These tasks formed the basis for standard work documentation, and instructional design principles enabled trainers to turn these tasks and skills into learning outcomes for training.

There are many instructional design models used across various industries, but they do share some common characteristics. Many are iterative processes, such as ADDIE (Hodell 2006) and the Dick and Carey Model (2009). Most of the models involve analysis and evaluation steps that inform learning design and assessment; for example, backward design (Wiggins and McTighe 2005) and Cathy Moore's action mapping. An initial analysis step can involve evaluating learners' skills and training needs, examining the organization's goals and any gaps or areas for improvement, and identifying problems to solve. Not every problem can be solved with training, and it is important to eliminate issues of motivation, physical environment, corporate culture, or knowledge gaps. For example, employees may be repeating mistakes that a job aid or cheat sheet could fix, or there could be inefficiencies due to the physical arrangement of the work space.

If the initial analysis has revealed gaps in identified skills, then those skills can inform the development of learning outcomes and training plans. Most learning outcomes follow a kind of formula, inspired by Robert Mager's 1962 book *Preparing Instructional Objectives*. They answer the question: "What does right look like?" One method for learning outcomes involves the mnemonic ABCD: Audience, Behavior, Condition, Degree (see figure 0.1 for examples).

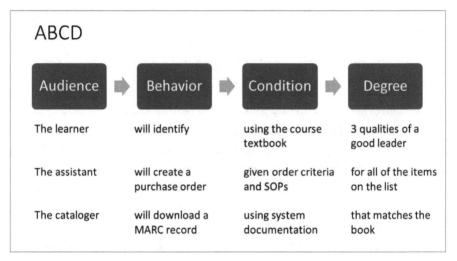

FIGURE 0.1
ABCD learning outcome examples

Another mnemonic for learning outcomes is SMART: Specific, Measurable, Attainable/Achievable, Relevant, Time-bound (Chatterjee and Corral 2017). For example:

> *By the end of this training (Time-bound), the learner will be able to describe (Specific, Measurable) the process for setting holdings in OCLC (Attainable/ Achievable, Relevant).*

Here is an example of a learning outcome that is not SMART:

> *The learner will understand cataloging.*

While the overall goal of training may be for employees to understand the fundamental functions of their department, understanding itself cannot be measured. How would anyone know whether someone understands cataloging? It can help to think of things (tasks, skills, observable behaviors) that successful catalogers can do—and then ask, what does successful cataloging look like? A successful cataloger might be able to find a matching MARC record for an item, transcribe an item's title with correct capitalization and punctuation, or add a Cutter number to a call number. This kind of analysis can lead to a SMART learning outcome such as:

> *At the end of the training, the cataloger will use matching record documentation to select and export OCLC records.*

Following these principles will lead more readily to success because learners will better understand what is expected of them, what they will be able to accomplish through learning, and how they might be evaluated. Writing learning outcomes as part of an overall strategy for learning in technical services will also help managers, supervisors, and trainers develop documentation (including training materials), and could also be a part of job classification or employee evaluation.

This book contains multiple examples of how TWI, lean management, instructional design, and other strategies can be used in training in cataloging, acquisitions, e-resources management, circulation, digitization, and preparation for a library service platform migration. (Almost all the examples in this book focus on a migration from a previously used platform to Ex Libris's Alma.) The editors' goal was to collect different training methodologies and case studies in order to offer technical services managers and trainers useful examples for creating a learning culture in their departments. The book's chapters cover academic and public libraries and consortia and are an indication that training needs are universal across different types of libraries and departments.

The book starts with two chapters ("Growing a Technical Services Learning Culture at NC State University Libraries" and "Establishing a Positive Training Culture") that discuss not specific training projects, but the importance of creating a positive training culture. The term *culture* is key here because the success of training is contingent on its collaborative and supportive nature. Learning can occur in many different ways, and in addition to improving quality and increasing productivity, it helps to build bridges and form cross-departmental relationships. Laura Sill's chapter on the community of practice model is one example of how to establish an organization-wide learning community around metadata work.

The potential approaches to training discussed in the book—Deming, just-in-time management, Vygotsky's scaffolded approach, information literacy concepts—all emphasize the same elements: identifying and creating training opportunities, deliberately incorporating training into everyday workflows, and selecting and using appropriate training methods (structured courses, lectures, micro-learning, self-directed learning, cross-training, hands-on practice, etc.). Identifying the staff's gaps in skills and knowledge is often a first step in any training effort. A few chapters address using industry core competencies in defining skill gaps and training needs ("Growing a Technical Services Learning Culture," "Mind the [Training] Gap," "Training Tech Services Using Concepts from Information Literacy Instruction"). Depending on their particular needs, some chapter authors selected different approaches, which ranged from creating a comprehensive in-house course on cataloging ("Practicing Partnerships") to providing micro-learning opportunities as a response to problems with help desk tickets or e-mail questions ("Just-in-Time Training").

Documentation is a key component of a learning culture. Many chapters of this book demonstrate that successful training is impossible without a strong emphasis on current, up-to-date, and complete documentation ("Technical Services Staff Training and Documentation during and after a Transition from Voyager to Alma"). Examples of a course curriculum ("Practicing Partnerships"), lesson plans ("Establishing a Positive Training Culture," "Cross-Organizational Learning through a Community of Practice"), and workflows and procedures ("Reactive and Proactive Approaches in the Training Program") are included throughout the book to make it practical and usable in real-life training projects.

The importance of using available technological and project management tools to organize the training is evident throughout the book. Several chapters describe using Trello, MS Teams, Zoom, and learning management systems to deliver training and monitor progress. The use of Trello for tracking cataloging training progress ("Looking Back to Move Forward") and for student training and management ("Reinvention of Student Worker Training") shows that it could be a versatile and flexible tool that is adaptable to many different contexts. A learning management system with capabilities for self-graded assessment and participation tracking can be used to deliver both a comprehensive cataloging course ("Practicing Partnerships") and circulation services training ("Circulation Services Training in a Remote Work Environment"). Zoom and MS Teams are just a few of the many different tools that are used to collaborate or deliver training virtually.

The book includes several examples of theoretical approaches and practical strategies. What emerges from each and every chapter, however, is the integral role that training plays in the success of technical service departments and libraries in general.

The editors hope that the following chapters provide useful information to all types of libraries and help with organizing successful training on a departmental, library-wide, or consortial level.

REFERENCES

Chatterjee, Debnath, and Janet Corral. 2017. "How to Write Well-Defined Learning Objectives." *Journal of Education in Perioperative Medicine* 19, no. 4.

Dick, Walter, James O. Carey, and Lou Carey. 2009. *The Systematic Design of Instruction*. 7th edition. Upper Saddle River, NJ: Merrill Pearson.

Graupp, Patrick, and Robert J. Wrona. 2016. *The TWI Workbook: Essential Skills of Supervisors*. Boca Raton, FL: CRC.

Hodell, Chuck. 2006. *ISD from the Ground Up: A No-Nonsense Approach to Instructional Design*. 2nd edition. American Society for Training and Development.

Mager, Robert Frank. 1962. *Preparing Instructional Objectives*. Belmont, CA: Fearon Publishers.

Moore, Cathy. n.d. "Training Design—Cathy Moore." https://blog.cathy-moore .com/.

Wiggins, Grant, and Jay McTighe. 2005. *Understanding by Design*. Alexandria, VA: Association for Supervision & Curriculum Development.

Growing a Technical Services Learning Culture at NC State University Libraries

Beth Ashmore, Maria Collins, Xiaoyan Song, and Lynn Whittenberger

OVER THE PAST TWO DECADES, TECHNICAL SERVICES AT NORTH CAROLINA State University Libraries (hereafter, NC State Libraries, or the Libraries) have evolved quickly due to changing work and reductions in staff. In addition, the increased need for effective electronic resources management ushered in a new work culture characterized by automation and system-driven support. Establishing strategies for continuous learning to meet these challenges was a critical factor in developing a resilient staff able to respond to changes not only in the work itself but in their approach to work. Due in part to North Carolina State University's training efforts, staff have learned to approach their jobs as problem-solvers, and they are willing to tackle a larger portion of the resource life cycle rather than just serving as functional experts on more narrow tasks or processes. The strategies discussed in this chapter, such as cross-training, exposure training, targeted learning, informal training, core competencies training, learning groups, and cross-unit teams, have created a pathway for building a continuous learning culture that has enabled staff to adapt and make quick changes within a supportive framework rather than a fearful one.

CROSS-TRAINING

The technical services operations at NC State Libraries merged in June 2011 to form a single department, Acquisitions & Discovery (A&D). A&D staff are responsible for all aspects of acquisitions, serials management, cataloging, electronic resources management, database maintenance, and metadata services. One of the key components of the merger was cross-training for all staff. Catalogers learned acquisitions work and vice versa. To prepare for cross-training, managers held focus groups to identify questions to address, workflows affected, and action items or intended outcomes. (See figure 1.1 for an example of a focus group's charge.) All staff participated in multiple focus groups, which were successful in getting them involved in conceptualizing and visualizing upcoming changes in their work. This participatory process eased staff fears and resulted in collated decisions and recommendations for each of the various areas affected by the merger.

A training team was identified to create department-wide training content for cross-training all staff. Responsibility for the delivery of this content was divided among the members of the training team. Staff members with expertise in the areas identified for training were then asked to lead small groups that facilitated and provided support for practice activities. Consequently, a significant number of staff participated in leading aspects of the cross-training. Dedicated time was taken each week for staff to participate in both training sessions and group activities, so the pace of training was intense and occurred over the course of a year. These training sessions proved critical in establishing a knowledge baseline that created consistency and allowed staff to quickly adjust to their new work assignments resulting from the merger. These efforts also normalized regular delivery and participation in training throughout the department. Positioning learning as a foundational work activity allowed management to continue training beyond the initial merger and cross-training period.

EXPOSURE LEARNING

A&D managers also deployed lightweight learning strategies such as exposure learning to introduce new ideas and trends to the department. A&D defines exposure learning as learning about library topics that currently do not impact daily work but have the potential to impact technical services work in the future. The NC State Libraries provide funding for staff development, which department heads can request. To support exposure learning, A&D encourages staff to be on the lookout for learning opportunities, and if something looks

Project Summary

Goal: Perform an environmental scan of all of the ways serial physical materials enter, move through, and exit Acquisitions and Discovery (A&D) and the rest of technical services. Information gathered will be used to inform the creation of a workflow map that will then be used to make decisions on the handoff of materials in transitioned unit work and at Hunt Library.

Initial Questions

1. Where is material located before it enters A&D?
2. Where is material located after it exits A&D?
3. Where does material live at each stage of the workflow?
4. How does the material move within each unit (Acquisitions vs. Cataloging)?
5. How does the material move between each unit (Acquisitions vs. Cataloging), i.e., what are the handoff points?
6. Who is responsible for each movement?

Workflows Addressed

- Journals
- Standing orders and continuations
- Serial life cycle management, including new orders, cancellations, cessations, bibliographic changes, etc.

Focus Group

- Project manager—Serials Specialist
- Group members—Technician Journey (Serials), Technician Advanced (Preservation), Technician Journey (Preservation), Technician Advanced (Serials)

FIGURE 1.1
Example of a focus group's charge to assist with the merger of operations

interesting, to share information on the opportunity with their supervisor. If the department head agrees that the topic looks promising, a request will be submitted to the Libraries for funding. All A&D staff are invited to participate in these learning opportunities. Generally, the A&D Department has tended to register for webinar presentations or workshops, as these provide the broadest opportunity for participation, and recordings of them are usually provided that can be shared internally. A&D keeps a local file of archived recordings that staff can view at their convenience. Past exposure learning topics have included linked data, programming languages and technologies, and alternative metadata schemas.

TARGETED TRAINING OR LEARNING

When staff need additional skills or knowledge to be successful in their work, their manager will often create a targeted training plan. Typically, targeted training is spurred by changes in the technical services environment (RDA, for example). The authors have found that targeted training is most successful when there are clearly stated expectations for participation and managers are prepared to shift, delay, or otherwise manage staff workloads when all or part of a staff member's workday is devoted to training and learning. In the past, selected staff would meet as a unit or group for training together. This had the benefit of colleagues being able to assist and support each other as a learning cohort. Examples of targeted training topics have included cataloging with RDA and using MarcEdit.

INFORMAL TRAINING

Probably the most common type of training in the department is informal training, or the apprenticeship approach. As a need arises for training on a particular task, staff who are experienced or skilled in that task will provide an informal training session for the staff member requiring that information. A&D management has encouraged staff to take on trainer roles, creating documentation on process and delivering one-on-one or small-group training as needed. Management supports staff that take on training roles by adjusting work assignments for the duration of the training and by recognizing training work done or new skills learned in staff members' annual appraisals. Any documentation created for training is retained in our department's shared Google Drive and may also be linked to on our internal wiki for future reference. Informal training examples include batch record loading and electronic theses cataloging.

CORE COMPETENCIES TRAINING

The cross-training that followed the department merger revealed several gaps in the department's previous approach to training. A reliance on informal or ad hoc training mostly for new staff had resulted in inconsistent knowledge and practice. The cross-training efforts after the merger created a shared understanding of accepted practices in the department, which resulted in improved communication and efficiencies. Following this experience, A&D supervisors decided to take a more thoughtful approach to training by analyzing the different types of training needed by the department, which primarily fell into two different camps—training requiring a systematic and cyclical approach, and one-off training that could be provided at the point of need. In addition, managers also needed to identify future job skills required for carrying out ever-changing technical services work, such as quality control work for automated processes and query writing to manage and analyze data outputs.

In an effort to identify current and future training needs as well as design a cohesive training framework that would address the need for more systematic and cyclical training, a team of A&D managers was charged with evaluating core competencies from a variety of relevant professional organizations, such as the American Library Association and NASIG. Through an analysis of these core competencies, the group evaluated what skills the department needed, who needed them, and how to create learning programs to ensure both competency and continued development in those areas. The department chose to review seven core competencies documents relevant to the department's core work:

- LLAMA Foundational Competencies (ALA)
- Core Competencies for Cataloging and Metadata Professional Librarians (ALA)
- New Skillset for Metadata Management (OCLC)
- Linked Data Competency Index (LD4PE)
- Core Competencies for Electronic Resources Librarians (NASIG)
- Core Competencies for Scholarly Communication Librarians (NASIG)
- Core Competencies for Acquisitions Professionals (ALA)

The individual skills and competencies in these documents were first categorized according to broad skills or knowledge sets, including both soft- and domain-skill designations such as communication or metadata assessment. The individual competencies were also categorized by their importance to the department, the staff positions that had the skill, the number of staff who needed the skill, and additional training needs (see figure 1.2).

The categorization helped to identify common themes in soft-skill areas like communication, customer service, and project management, as well as domain knowledge areas like metadata, financial data, and technology. Scoring the importance of a skill, as well as the number of department members who needed a certain skill, helped to identify future training work for the department. With all of this information, the management team spun off a smaller training team to identify immediate areas to address and the resources needed to provide training, including internal workshops, webinar recordings, outside

FIGURE 1.2
Example of categorized core competencies

Category	Source	Skill or Knowledge	
Communication & relationship	LLAMA Foundational Competencies	Communication skills	
Domain knowledge: metadata	Core Competencies for Cataloging and Metadata Professional Librarians	Ability to create and edit consistent data; understanding of the importance of data standardization	
Domain knowledge: data management service	OCLC New Skillset for Metadata Management	Management of research data	
Domain knowledge: linked data	Linked Data Competency Index	Knows the subject-predicate-object component structure of a triple	
Domain knowledge: systems and tools	Core Competencies for E-Resources Librarians	Technology: knowledge of standards, protocols, and structures (IP, FTP, OpenURL/z39.50, Shibboleth, OAI-PMH, EDI)	

speakers, and online training tools like LinkedIn Learning. With regard to department-wide training, the first topic chosen was change management. This topic was selected as a way to set the stage and prepare the staff for ongoing training activities. The team provided the staff with short readings, a list of training videos from LinkedIn Learning, and an asynchronous exercise to prepare staff for an in-person workshop on change management. Unfortunately, due to the COVID-19 pandemic, the change management training was postponed. The pandemic provided great lessons in change management in real time, demonstrating how capable department staff are at managing change, learning new skills, and thriving in complicated times. As work schedules stabilize, the training team will begin to tackle creating a systematic training schedule for core competencies that fall within domain-specific areas.

Importance to A&D	Who has it?	Who needs it?	Training Schedule
5. Very important	Everyone	Everyone	Continuous
5. Very important	Dept. catalogers / database maintenance people	Dept. catalogers / database maintenance people	Onboarding & periodic for new standards and systems
2. A little important	Some librarians	Anyone who partners with Research Facilitation Services	Periodic training as part of Research Facilitation Services partnership
3. Somewhat important	Librarians working on Linked Data projects	Anyone who serves on a linked data project	Possible exposure training for all; periodic professional development for Linked Data team
4. Important	Librarians	Librarians	Periodic training as new standards and tools are implemented

LEARNING GROUPS

In addition to planned learning opportunities, there are often training topics that evolve on their own through staff needs or interests. Learning groups are one way A&D has responded to supporting those educational interests. Typically, a learning group has been created by a member of A&D who has an interest in a topic, and who has gotten support for group development from their supervisor and the head of A&D. The group then forms organically, through an open call for participation, usually an e-mail sent to the department and any other interested parties. One current example is our Python learning group. Python is a popular programming language in the acquisitions and metadata communities, and a number of staff and librarians in the department were independently investigating how they might use Python to improve existing automation and develop ways to further automate the department's processes. Led by Xiaoyan Song, electronic resources librarian for A&D, the Python learning group was created as a cohort learning group to give individuals with an interest in developing Python skills a place to get together and share their projects and learning resources and support each other. The group even attracted members from other departments within the Libraries. The group's members also presented a session to the department on what they learned, and the skills they developed while working together.

Learning a new task can be difficult to fit into an already packed schedule, no matter how valuable that new skill may ultimately be. By creating a structure like a learning group to support a common interest, staff have hopefully found it easier to dedicate time and prioritize the development of those skills, as well as inspire one another.

CROSS-UNIT TEAMS

Now that the A&D Department is ten years out from the 2011 merger, some of the flexibility gained from the initial cross-training has lessened. Although this is likely a normal reaction as people's roles stabilize, it does create a barrier to change. As a means of establishing a more fluid and nimble approach to working across unit lines in the department, A&D has begun the process of creating and implementing cross-unit teams. In addition to addressing the need to create a flexible organizational structure for the department, these teams allow the department to provide dedicated support to areas of growth as well as problem areas. These teams are designed to address several challenges:

- They allow staff from different units to work and learn together, thus breaking down unit-specific boundaries.
- They allow staff to use their domain expertise on new areas or problems outside of technical services.
- They allow staff to broaden their work experience and gain new skills.
- They allow technical services staff to more readily partner with stakeholders across the Libraries.

This last purpose is especially critical because it pushes staff toward a more outward-facing technical services approach, one in which staff are essentially using honed skill sets for performing traditional technical services work in new or nontraditional areas across the Libraries. This has smoothed the way for technical services staff to offer consultation services and support for other units in the Libraries.

A&D was asked by the Libraries administration to provide twenty hours a week in support of the Libraries' statistical data work, so A&D managers decided to use this request to pilot the idea for A&D's first cross-unit team. This enabled A&D to pull staff from multiple units to support this work. Two team leads were identified to pull together a charge for the group and form an implementation and training plan. The team leads are also responsible for project management and communication. The pilot team, called the Library Impact Analysis cross-unit team, supports the Organizational Strategy Department in the collecting, cleaning, and reporting of statistics. In its initial stages, this team identified a number of areas for training. Some of these areas were specific to using tools for data collection, and only those who would be executing that data would require that training. Other skills, like new Excel skills for aggregating and visualizing data, have potential applications in regular A&D work and will be shared throughout the cross-unit team. As the team develops and assists with more bespoke data and visualization requests, the team looks forward to using new tools like Datawrapper and Tableau and being able to bring those skills back to the rest of the department to share, either through workshops or through learning groups.

Other cross-unit teams are in various stages of implementation. These include:

ILS Audit: This team will identify, evaluate, and maintain the integrity of the data curated by A&D in the ILS suite of systems.

ERM Strategy: This team will evaluate and define a unified strategy and establish priorities for electronic resources management for A&D.

Website Metadata: This team will support the work of A&D that intersects with the Libraries' website.

A&D Statistics: This team will facilitate and coordinate communication for the collection, management, and display of departmental statistics.

Special Collections: This team will provide support to A&D's collaborations with Special Collections.

Project Management: This team will establish best practices and provide project management support.

These teams will also form a communication plan to follow to ensure that direct supervisors are kept in the loop about resource needs. Even with just a few of these teams deployed, A&D has noticed increased interactions with stakeholders, as well as improved redundancy and knowledge retention within the department when staff have left the organization, both of which are important when onboarding and training new staff.

CONCLUDING THOUGHTS

Overall, A&D's multifaceted approach to learning has resulted in a technical services department that embraces a learning culture where staff feel comfortable both in delivering and in receiving training, and where staff recognize that learning new skills is part of their regular work. These strategies have contributed to a learning culture that allows A&D staff to succeed in responding quickly, adapting, and innovating in an ever-changing environment.

Establishing a Positive Training Culture

Hyun Chu Kim and Ariel Turner

THIS CASE STUDY ADDRESSES THE HISTORICAL CONTEXT OF DEVELOPING a positive training culture in the Technical Services unit at Kennesaw State University under the unit's strategic plan. It discusses how this culture allowed for the optimization of existing workflows, the development of new workflows, and the development of training and cross-training programs to support the strategic plan's goals. Numerous training opportunities have been created and provided to the unit, other library units, and library colleagues at other institutions during the past few years.

BACKGROUND

Kennesaw State University (KSU) is a comprehensive university and the second largest university in Georgia, with over 41,000 students. The university, a part of the University System of Georgia (USG), was consolidated in 2015 from two institutions, KSU and Southern Polytechnic State University. The university now has two campuses, and its student enrollment increases each year.

Between 2015 and 2018, the KSU Library System underwent two major system migrations. The first migration occurred as a result of the consolidation of the two universities into one. This migration required an extensive policy and functional review and assessment, a piloting phase for the new combined system, and data review and cleanup to prepare for the migration. After the migration, additional data review was necessary. The extensive system migration process necessitated teamwork, cross-training, and troubleshooting. The initial systems migration in 2015 ultimately helped to prepare the new consolidated system for a migration from Ex Libris Voyager to Ex Libris Alma two years later.

After the consolidation of the two library systems, USG institutions migrated from Voyager to Ex Libris Alma as the university system's next-generation library system. The migration to Alma was initiated and led by the state consortium, GALILEO Interconnected Libraries (GIL), and the multiyear process involved a statewide team of institutional leads functioning as project managers for each unique institution. The team leads coordinated statewide policy and procedural decision-making and technical setup for their respective instances of Alma. KSU established an implementation team. In order to ensure a smooth transition to the new system, intensive cross-training between library units was necessary in order to determine how to best set up the new system. This cross-training and inter-unit collaboration continued through the testing and implementation of Alma.

The Technical Services unit of the KSU Library System was deeply involved and affected by both the ILS consolidation in 2015 and the system migration in 2017. In addition to the challenges of systems migrations, other major changes occurred that impacted the Technical Services unit. KSU was reclassified as an R2 institution in late 2018. Before this, the KSU Library System was considered both a college and a department within the institution. Following the reclassification of KSU as an R2 institution and a system-wide comprehensive administrative review to streamline efficiencies, the library reorganized to better reflect the structure in traditional academic units as a college with two departments in July 2019. Two departments, Public Services and Library Resources, were created within the larger library system. Technical Services is now a unit under the Library Resources Department, along with two other units: Collection Development and Systems and Online Services.

The significant changes the unit has responded to over the past ten years underscore the unit's flexibility, innovation, and collaboration, as presented in strategic planning exercises within the department over the years. The need to review, revise, and develop workflows is consistently emphasized by unit members, as is the collaboration of Technical Services with other library units. While some of these challenges and the focus of collaboration are not unique to the KSU Technical Services unit, this background is an important factor when considering the development of a positive training culture in the unit.

LITERATURE REVIEW

Intner and Johnson (2008) identified a common stereotype of technical services staff as introverted and less outgoing and recommended that "good managers should designate themselves first on a list that includes the whole department staff to take responsibility for dispelling the stereotype" (120). Thus, it is important for leaders of technical services teams to actively work against any potential stereotypes of technical services staff as less willing to engage in collaborative work or teamwork with other units. In a 2017 survey of technical services librarians, nearly half of the respondents expressed a desire for an improvement in collaboration and communication with their counterparts in public services (Weng and Ackerman 2017, 204). This desire for increased collaboration, widely voiced by technical services librarians, reflects opportunities for innovation and cross-training not only within technical services teams but across library functional areas as well.

Technical services teams in academic libraries face persistent changes as new or modified acquisitions and metadata technology and applications are constantly being introduced, and best practices are adjusted accordingly. Dehmlow explains how the complexity of cataloging transitioned from "a single metadata format" to "multiple complex schemes" and how "acquisitions is pushing toward greater automation" (Dehmlow 2017, 4). The continuous nature of changes to technologies and workflows highlights the need for ongoing professional development for technical services librarians and staff.

Kidd (2010) discussed the Knowles theory that "adults approach learning as problem-solving" (217). The equation of learning with problem-solving is particularly relevant here because technical services librarians and paraprofessionals must continuously learn and expand their knowledge and skill sets in order to resolve any issues they encounter while performing their daily duties. As professionals, they often try to expand their skill set and search for opportunities for webinars or training that are discoverable via e-mails from the discussion lists of their interest groups, vendors, and others. For example, a survey by Tosaka and Park (2014) showed that 67.7 percent of the respondents'

RDA training consisted of being self-taught from LC online materials, such as webcasts or PowerPoint training materials, and 63.7 percent by webinars and other online training sessions, which are considered self-directed learning.

Ahlfeld (2010) explained how "a self-directed, exploration approach" enabled successful professional development with support from the administration in her case study. This emphasizes the need for administrative and organizational support even when self-directed learners are actively pursuing professional development opportunities (17). Dehmlow (2017) also emphasized the importance of "organizational commitment to training" as "technologically driven change regularly outpaces generational personnel turnover in libraries" (5). This research reflects both the ongoing need for professional development among technical services faculty and staff and the success of self-directed learning as an approach for adult learners in technical services roles.

The findings from the literature on the importance of collaboration for technical services faculty and staff, the initiative associated with adult learning theory, and the importance of organizational support for success are all supported by the authors' own observations on the training culture of Technical Services at KSU. As addressed in the next section, the Technical Services unit at KSU demonstrated an interest in collaboration, an ability to independently identify and pursue professional development opportunities, and the benefits of administrative support for professional development.

ONBOARDING

The need for continuous training and professional development for technical services staff and faculty, the importance of organizational support, and a desire for cross-training and collaboration across units have all influenced the development of a positive training culture in Technical Services at KSU. This culture begins with the onboarding process for new employees, which all members of the unit take part in. Beginning in 2017, new staff hires in the Technical Services unit have been onboarded using an intensive cross-training program for their first few weeks. Prior to each new hire's start date, a schedule is established in consultation with members of Technical Services so that every new member of the unit is offered an introduction to the work of each member of the unit. Further and more in-depth sessions are scheduled relevant to the new hire's area of focus within the unit. This approach to onboarding offers several benefits. New hires are better able to understand the bigger picture of how their work fits into the unit, the staff involved in the onboarding training develop confidence through repetition in introducing their work and its importance to the unit, and the process enables and encourages increased communication and unit cohesion.

COLLABORATING

Normalizing and encouraging collaboration both within and outside of the unit has also contributed to creating a positive training environment in Technical Services. Under the Technical Services strategic plan developed in 2017, optimizing existing workflows and creating new workflows to establish best practices for resource management were highlighted among the action steps to improve the discoverability of library resources, and this necessitated partnerships with and the involvement of staff in other units. Following the migration from Voyager to Alma, the need to streamline workflows became apparent, particularly in light of new procedures needed in the new system. Unlike Voyager, Alma is a cloud-based library services platform where different functional modules are interconnected. It requires users to have roles (instead of logging in to different modules) in order to perform their work in their areas of expertise. As the Technical Services unit updated its procedural documents and realized the impact of its work on other units in the new system, the need for greater collaboration between units emerged. One example of an interconnected process is the handling of books ordered as "shelf ready" from the library's primary vendor. Technical Services quickly discovered the need to collaborate with Access Services on handling shelf-ready books, since those books are shipped directly to two libraries on each campus instead of being delivered to Technical Services. Access Services could receive the books and shelve them when no cataloging errors were present, but work orders were created to transition books to Technical Services for those with any metadata mistakes.

Once the need for collaboration with other units was identified, Technical Services faculty and staff initiated meetings with other units to discuss the existing procedures and propose updated workflows (see figure 2.1).

Library Technical Services Acquisitions Procedures

Shelf-Ready Receiving Process

When a box of books has been received from GOBI, check the following items on the box:

- The label at the end of the box should show the correct subaccount, either for Johnson or for Sturgis.
- The UPS shipping label on top of the box should have the invoice number at the bottom of the label. (Please note: For multiple boxes received, group together boxes with the same invoice number(s) and follow receiving procedures for each group of boxes.)
- Check for the box with an INVOICE ENCLOSED stamp on the top.

After verifying information on the box, you may proceed to receiving the shelf-ready books as follows:

1. Open the box of books with INVOICE ENCLOSED stamped on it and remove the invoice.
   Please note: A TECH SERVICES invoice with processing fees may be included, so please just keep that with the invoice for the books and send to Technical Services when receiving has been complete.
2. Compare the invoice number on the paper invoice to the invoice number on the shipping label of the box to ensure they match.
3. Remove the books from the box and place in alphabetical order by title on a cart.
4. Beginning with the first book, perform the following steps:

FIGURE 2.1
Shelf-ready receiving process (Goodin 2017)

After reviewing the procedures together, Technical Services updated the procedural documents and provided training to colleagues in other units.

Technical Services also collaborates closely with the Collection Development unit to develop and refine the workflows for selection and monograph acquisition. Collection Development coordinates the selection of books through liaison assignments for library faculty who are tasked with selecting materials. This is accomplished by establishing monograph budgets, along with internal deadlines, to spend a certain percentage of each selector's allocated budget for the year. Collection Development also began hosting an annual "Purchasing Party," where the selectors gathered to work through collection development together and provide tips from the Collection Development and Acquisitions teams to make the selecting experience more fun and efficient. The acquisitions librarian and staff members attend the Purchasing Parties and provide answers to questions in order to clarify and select titles in the GOBI platform. Technical Services staff provide selection tips along with documentation, so that selectors can revisit the latter as needed to recollect. Some examples of the popular tips that selectors have appreciated are the "GOBI Selection Tips" and "Notify Selector Instructions" documents developed by Technical Services staff (see figure 2.2).

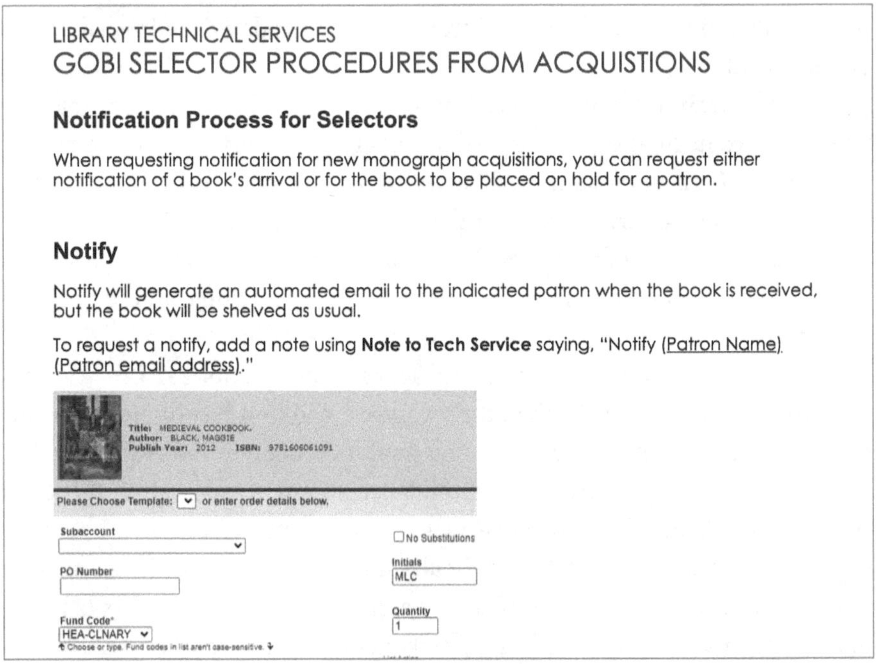

LIBRARY TECHNICAL SERVICES

GOBI SELECTOR PROCEDURES FROM ACQUISTIONS

Notification Process for Selectors

When requesting notification for new monograph acquisitions, you can request either notification of a book's arrival or for the book to be placed on hold for a patron.

Notify

Notify will generate an automated email to the indicated patron when the book is received, but the book will be shelved as usual.

To request a notify, add a note using **Note to Tech Service** saying, "Notify (Patron Name) (Patron email address)."

FIGURE 2.2
Notify Selector Instructions (Chatelain 2020)

CROSS-TRAINING

Another action step for the unit's strategic planning goals was to develop a cross-training program. This helped Technical Services increase the department's work capacity and flexibility. The Technical Services paraprofessionals were cross-trained on the other areas of expertise in the unit; for example, metadata assistants trained on ordering and receiving, and the acquisitions staff trained on cataloging. Non-metadata librarians from both Technical Services and other units of the library were cross-trained on cataloging. Some of the cross-training involved multiple days of cataloging training, including a presentation and hands-on cataloging, and a post-training review of the records that were cataloged for a month. This cataloging training was offered to a non-library unit, the department of Museum, Archives, and Rare Books. Technical Services librarians and staff also provided presentations and hands-on training to other library units on the shelf-ready receiving process. The success of the cross-training action step was evaluated quantitatively at the end of the year by the number of presentations provided, the number of individuals trained, and the procedural documents updated, and was found to be successful.

The cross-training (see figures 2.3 and 2.4) developed by Technical Services was then extended as a professional development opportunity to the rest of the library. When a new staff member or librarian outside of the unit is hired, Technical Services provides a general overview of the unit.

The general overview also provides an opportunity for library employees in other units to understand how Technical Services functions, and to appreciate the expertise of each member of the unit. In addition, Technical Services offers regular open sessions to help colleagues in other units learn about Technical Services functions. In the past few years, the unit has offered sessions on book repair, work orders, and Alma Analytics, open to interested parties. These sessions always draw strong attendance numbers and positive feedback from peers outside of Technical Services, which further facilitates a positive experience for the unit's staff and faculty and the ability to collaborate with other units. Due to the success of these sessions, the unit now offers training to both internal and external library stakeholders as appropriate, in order to increase collaboration and library support across both campuses.

FIGURE 2.3
Cross-training documents (Turner 2017)

Date Completed	Title	Links	Password	Time
		GOBI Training		
	GOBI Basics Recording: Part I	https://us.bbcollab.com/recording/D816CEDD2E7BA64C-FE89A7549F923C90	N/A	1 hour, 20 minutes
	Selecting Titles in GOBI using the Select Cart	https://www.youtube.com/watch?v=w12AktM-T3el&list=PLm0N-3NPJMzORf-Ez-vAVz6sPLfmdLaQLY&index=4	N/A	5 minutes
	Ordering Selected titles in using the Order Cart	https://www.youtube.com/watch?v=RiVN-8AQ2Th0&list=PLm0N-3NPJMzORf-Ez-vAVz6sPLfmdLaQLY&index=4&t=0s	N/A	6 minutes
	GobiTween	https://www.youtube.com/watch?v=5qkLecWX-28Q&list=PLm0N-3NPJMzORf-Ez-vAVz6sPLfmdLaQLY&index=7	N/A	4 minutes
	Rush Ordering	https://www.youtube.com/watch?v=Y-912QE_SkE&list=PLm0N-3NPJMz0Rf-	N/A	2 minutes
	Invoices and Statements	https://www.youtube.com/watch?v=M5LwTNwWu-pA&list=PLm0N-3NPJMzORf-Ez-vAVz6sPLfmdLaQLY&index=18	N/A	2 minutes
	Gobi Bookzone	https://www.youtube.com/watch?v=a-hYM49b9fVQ&list=PLm0N-3NP-JMzORf-EzvAVz6sPLfmdLaQLY&index=24	N/A	3 minutes
	GOBI API	https://www.screencast.com/t/5W-sEvaxn0mar	N/A	3 minutes

FIGURE 2.4
Training documents (Turner 2017)

Week 1			
Date	**Activity**	**Space**	**Facilitator(s)**
4-Jun	Supervisor Meeting/Overview	TS Conference Room	Facilitator A
4-Jun	Tour of T/Settle In		Facilitator A
5-Jun	Leading from the Middle	KSU Center	Facilitator B
6-Jun	Introduction to Acquisitions/ Serials		Facilitator A
7-Jun	TS Request Form/Drive/ SharePoint	CP209B	Facilitator B
8-Jun	Johnson for AS	Johnson Library	
Week 2			
Date	**Activity**	**Space**	**Facilitator(s)**
11-Jun	Receiving/Serials	CP209A, Cube E	Facilitator C
12-Jun	Leading from the Middle	KSU Center	Facilitator B
13-Jun	Introduction to Cataloging	CP209C	Facilitator D
14-Jun	GOBI & Placing Orders Overview	CP209A, Cube B	Facilitator E
15-Jun	Johnson for AS	Johnson Library	
Week 3			
Date	**Activity**	**Space**	**Facilitator(s)**
18-Jun	Overview of Invoicing, Supplies Inventory	CP209A, Cube A	Facilitator F
18-Jun	Leading from the Middle	Sturgis 125	Facilitator B
19-Jun	Introduction to Processing	CP209A, Cube D	Facilitator G
20-Jun	Work Orders	CP209A, Cube E	Facilitator H
21-Jun	Discovery/E-Access Work	CP209D	Facilitator I
Week 4			
Date	**Activity**	**Space**	**Facilitator(s)**
25-Jun	Register for ePro Training	Online	KSU Procurement
26-Jun	OwlPay for Requesters	Online	KSU Procurement
27-Jun	Leading from the Middle	KSU Center	CUL Staff
28-Jun	Crisis Coordinator/Safety as TS/ Repository	CP 209	
29-Jun	Johnson for AS	Johnson Library	

ADMINISTRATIVE SUPPORT

An important factor in the establishment of a positive training culture has been support from the library administration. Librarians and staff are regularly offered opportunities to practice giving conference presentations within the comfort of library-hosted practice sessions. These sessions provide a safe place for library employees not only to practice but to learn from each other, thus fostering future potential areas for collaboration and cross-departmental work. Additional support from the library administration is provided in the form of funding professional development requests. Technical Services faculty and staff at KSU regularly identify areas for professional growth to understand and improve workflows, such as reviewing documentation or attending conferences and webinars. They communicate their interests or needs through a systematic process of submitting professional development requests. These requests are approved systematically through the library administration. This process of approving self-directed requests has been utilized successfully in our organization. The request form has been modified several times for efficient communications. These self-identified requests for professional development function similarly to the aforementioned cross-departmental workflow assessment and improvement. When library faculty and staff identify the need to improve workflows or procedures, they initiate training and update procedural documents. The initiative taken by Technical Services faculty and staff in the areas of professional development, cross-training, and workflow development reflects their comfort with continuous learning, and a positive training culture overall.

OUTCOMES

The positive training culture within Technical Services has enabled the unit to streamline existing workflows and develop new ones within the unit and across multiple departments. Technical Services has improved the documenting and sharing of new and updated procedures. The development of training and cross-training programs to support strategic goals, and the number of training sessions provided by Technical Services librarians and staff have been other valuable outcomes of the culture. There is increased collaboration with other library units to provide training. As a result, the number of training opportunities created and provided to the team, other library units, and library colleagues at other institutions during the past few years has expanded. This culture has also allowed Technical Services faculty and staff to expand their knowledge and expertise in their specialized areas. Professional development is evidenced by an increase in the number of presentations made by Technical Services librarians and staff at local conferences. The Technical Services staff's participation increased from zero in 2014 to an average of two staff presentations in 2018 and 2019. According to the recent annual library report gathered from self-reported data, five library staff presented at conferences in 2020 and three library staff in 2021, even during the pandemic. About 80 percent of Technical Services library staff are enrolled either in an MLIS program or other degree programs. The results of this cultural shift are confirmed by library-wide assessment. According to the data provided by the assessment and user experience librarian, "the number of faculty and staff who attended state, national, and international conferences, trainings, and workshops grew from 46 in FY 2018 to 55 this year, FY 2020. This has remained steady at almost 70% of the library personnel" (Manda Sexton, e-mail message to authors, July 28, 2021).

CONCLUSION

Significant changes in systems, organizational structure, and institutional needs revealed a need for increased collaboration, cross-training, and professional development for members of the KSU Technical Services unit. As observed in the literature, technical services staff and faculty strive for more collaboration with other library employees and find continuous professional development to be a necessary part of their work. Adult learning theory posits that a self-directed learning approach is most effective for adults who are seeking to develop professionally. These findings in the literature are supported by the authors' own observations of the positive training culture established at KSU; staff and faculty in the Technical Services unit regularly cross-train and collaborate with others outside of the unit, and regularly pursue professional development opportunities independently. The outcomes of developing and fostering a positive training culture include an increase in cross-training sessions, the development of workflow documentation, and an increase in professional presentations by staff empowered by their ability to train colleagues and pursue their own professional development. Areas of future research include a qualitative study of staff perceptions of training culture or a study of the perceptions of other units on cross-unit collaboration.

REFERENCES

Ahlfeld, Kelly. 2010. "Hands-On Learning with a Hands-Off Approach for Professional Development." *School Library Monthly* 26, no. 6: 16–18.

Chatelain, Michelle. 2020. "Notify Selector Instructions." Procedural document, Kennesaw State University, Georgia.

Dehmlow, Mark. 2017. "Editorial Board Thoughts: Reinvesting in Our Traditional Personnel through Knowledge Sharing and Training." *Information Technology & Libraries* 36, no. 4 (December): 4–6. doi: 10.6017/ital.v36i4.10239.

Goodin, Rick. 2017. "Shelf-Ready Receiving Process." Procedural document, Kennesaw State University, Georgia.

———. 2020. "Training Material." Training PowerPoint, Kennesaw State University, Georgia.

Intner, Sheila S., and Peggy Johnson. 2008. *Fundamentals of Technical Services Management*. ALA Fundamentals Series. Chicago: American Library Association.

Kennesaw State University. "About Kennesaw State University." www.kennesaw.edu/about/.

Kidd, Terry T. 2010. *Online Education and Adult Learning: New Frontiers for Teaching Practices*. Hershey, PA: IGI Global.

Knowles, Malcolm S. 1976. "The Future Role of Libraries in Adult Education." *Southeastern Librarian* 75 (January): 43–47.

———. 1984. *Andragogy in Action*. Jossey-Bass Management Series. Jossey-Bass.

Tosaka, Yuji, and Jung-ran Park. 2014. "RDA: Training and Continuing Education Needs in Academic Libraries." *Journal of Education for Library & Information Science* 55, no. 1: 3–25.

Turner, Ariel. 2017. "Cross-Training Plan for New Hires." Internal training schedule, Kennesaw State University, Georgia.

Weng, Cathy, and Erin Ackerman. 2017. "Towards Sustainable Partnership: Examining Cross-Perceptions of Public and Technical Services Academic Librarians." *Library Resources & Technical Services* 61, no. 4: 198–211. doi: 10.5860/lrts.61n4.198.

3

A Deming Approach to Training in Technical Services

Kristy White and John White

TECHNICAL SERVICES (TS), WHILE DEFINED DIFFERENTLY AT DIFFERENT libraries, are always essential to the ever-changing organizational structures of libraries in the twenty-first century. Consequently, understanding the workflows in technical services, ongoing assessment of their adequacy to the goals of the library or organization, and efficient adaptation to new organizational designs are all part of building an effective TS department.

One potentially fruitful approach to developing an effective TS department is the application of W. E. Deming's work in organizational management to training and the administration of technical services. Deming's methods and models of management involve analyzing the state of current knowledge and practice in a department, building and expanding on that knowledge base, and fostering effective adaptation based on new knowledge and improved organizational structures. The Deming cycle synthesizes information into manageable bites, encouraging a measured and incremental acquisition of skills, along with the ability to manipulate tasks, to create increased efficiency and a broad streamlining of productivity, even in the midst of budgetary or other crises, such as having to go completely online due to a pandemic. Furthermore, approaching TS systems from the standpoint of the Deming cycle encourages a consistent and ongoing consciousness of, and reflection on, system processes by all members of any given system, promoting both a richer understanding of the system as a whole and one's place in it, and potentially resulting in an improved and more focused approach to team member training.

This chapter will discuss in broad terms some of the essential shifts and changes occurring and likely to occur in the future in technical services departments. Secondly, it will sketch the basic premises of the Deming approach to management, with a particular emphasis on the nature and value of the Deming cycle for TS training. Finally, it will illustrate some ways in which applying the Deming cycle to TS can aid innovation and effectiveness.

TECHNICAL SERVICES, TODAY AND TOMORROW

Changes in the work of traditional technical services have underlined the need for a continuous reassessment of workflows and an intentional, informed, and ongoing adaptive process, due both to increased technological capabilities and to correspondingly increasing expectations from users. Furthermore, these changes require consistent and continuous training for both new and seasoned team members, something that is required by technological changes but which also adds value to TS departments.

Libraries and librarians have struggled for many years with an identity crisis of sorts because changes in the publishing industry, technological advances, and subsequent changes in user behavior have reshaped the landscape of information and access. Moreover, technical services have been additionally challenged in some ways and too often dismissed as not intellectual or necessary to fulfill scholars' needs when compared to front-line public services (Laskowski and Maddox Abbott 2014, 13).

These developments call for an efficient and streamlined approach when we respond to the new possibilities in technical services, while simultaneously being sensitive to our library's and organization's missions, and the existing strategic planning in them. "Library administrators [must] try to find ways to meet these challenges by transforming and streamlining workflows and prioritizing objectives through their strategic planning processes and other mechanisms" (Davis 2016, 52).

There is no reason to think that such demands will change anytime soon because all the same factors that are currently driving the changes in technical services appear set to continue into the indefinite future. Furthermore, TS departments in particular require continuous and intentional training of team members because of the specific confluence of challenges faced by library administrations, such as increased demands in the face of decreasing budgets, the constant evolution of technology, and the changing formats available for purchase. "The major shift from print to electronic resources (e-resources), including born-digital resources, in library collections over the last decade has impacted every area in academic libraries" (Davis 2016, 52).

TS departments must therefore be vigilant in their understanding of available resources and consistently use ongoing training and adaptation in order to maintain the highest level of service to the library and its users. Libraries and library departments will "need leadership that inspires innovation and that encourages us to learn from both our successes and mistakes" (Davis 2016, 64). Technical services will need to continue to adapt just as quickly as the technology evolves, in order to meet those changing needs. If anything, the pandemic has only highlighted this situation. With the various changes occurring in TS, more and more responsibility for privacy control, licensing agreements, and ethical decision-making comes into play (White and White 2021). The consistent and ongoing analysis and improvement of processes, as well as ongoing education and training in those processes, are crucial for the efficiency and effectiveness of the TS department because the change from print to electronic has made TS, if anything, even more important to library functioning and success than it has been in the past.

THE DEMING CYCLE

W. Edwards Deming was an influential management theorist who is sometimes referred to as the "father of management theory." He is best known for his outstanding work in the post–World War II era, when he aided a devastated Japanese industrial base in its transformation to become a world-class industrial power. Deming's original and innovative view of how organizations work most efficiently, sometimes referred to as the "high-performance" management style, especially impacted the Japanese auto industry and, in part due to the latter's success, has extended into many other areas, including education and libraries. For the purposes of this chapter, it will be sufficient to just give a bird's-eye overview of the Deming approach and then focus on one of the immediately relevant aspects of his theory, the Deming cycle.

The high-performance management style is a systems approach (Kriemadis 2018, 101–2). This is to say that the high-performance style is not based solely on outcomes, as perhaps the majority of American management styles are. It assumes that the vast majority of poor outcomes are due not to problems or failures in this or that single factor, or in a team member, but are the result of poor or inadequate system design in general or specific problems within a system, such as a lack of adequate training. Deming claimed that statistical analyses of organizational systems typically show that even when, say, a particular team member is less than stellar at their job, the team member is still within the statistical range of adequate system functioning. In many cases, therefore, the manager should not simply assume this team member is a "weak link" but that there is inefficiency in the design of the system, and that the failure to fit the system and the team members in the most effective way, and/or the failure to train team members in the best and most up-to-date ways, are most likely what is inhibiting the best outcomes (Deming 1986).

Thus, a primary goal of management, one might say, is to analyze and modify the system being managed, and try to make the whole system as efficient and effective in the production of quality services as possible. This includes putting team members in situations most conducive to their strengths, and investing in their ongoing education and training. However, the Deming approach also assumes that management systems alone will not do the trick. Any improvement in management systems must have—as more or less exact correlates—the aims of improving technology and developing an up-to-date system for training team members. Improved technologies require investment on the part of organizations in team members and a consistent, ongoing regimen of training.

For reasons like these, Deming considered the standard annual personnel evaluation an example of a potentially destructive device for any organization, since it focuses on blaming rather than training individuals, and makes team members fear for their jobs and reluctant to highlight problems in the system, lest they themselves be blamed for the system's faults—an outstanding recipe for assuring no improvement in the organization's status quo.

One of the consequences of Deming's approach is that it deemphasizes the hierarchical management style so typical of American organizational practice in favor of a shared responsibility for effectiveness, efficiency, and quality control among all team members. In certain respects, the manager is more like a coach than a boss (White 2021), is in close communication with team members, and is in the business of educating, training, and building trusting relationships with them. The Deming approach both values team members' experience and expects all team members to participate in the process of analyzing and improving efficiency and quality in an ongoing way (White 2021). This process can succeed only if all team members are committed to efficiency, effectiveness, and quality products or services (Kriemadis 2018, 86), and can feel certain that their observations on system inefficiencies will not be held against them. In this model, the intelligent organization invests both time and money in the ongoing training of team members and considers its employees to be assets worthy of such investment, rather than as liabilities or as unfortunate sources of expense. The Deming cycle is a case in point of this model.

Deming's simplified version of this cycle is commonly called PDCA (later PDSA):

1. *Plan:* Describe (or revise) the components of the business process with the goal of improving results.
2. *Do:* Implement the revised plan or process and then measure its performance.
3. *Check (Study):* Assess the measurements and report the results to decision-makers.
4. *Act:* Decide on changes needed to improve the process. Cycle through the process again, as needed (Kriemadis 2018, 99–100).

This model uses a systems approach, one which assumes that one must describe, measure, and assess the effectiveness of any given system in all its parts. Implicit in this approach, in fact, is that the goal of any organization should not be short-term benefits or profits but long-term and consistent improvement (Deming 1986). It also assumes that team members are valued, experienced parts of the system, and have perhaps the most important and most comprehensive point of view on their own part in the system. Indeed, responsibility for the first three steps of this process are worked through by the entire team, especially those who are "on the ground" and have the most relevant and up-to-date experience. Their full participation is necessary and important for both describing and measuring the efficiency of the processes. Finally, the model assumes that much of the improvement in system functioning is the result of improved technology, which in turn requires that team members are consistently educated and trained so as to make the most out of the technological advances. The goal of improving the system's efficiency and effectiveness is therefore in large measure a function of adequate training.

Implementing the Deming cycle not only makes possible further growth and development among participants, but it encourages participants to consistently analyze, develop, and implement changes in the processes themselves, without the fear that greater efficiency might be at odds with them continuing in their own jobs. Such an approach can only work to the extent that team members can feel confident that their experience and insight matter to management, and that management's decisions to change and improve systems will include ongoing training.

One of the authors of this chapter has previously argued that mapping workflows is a valuable tool for implementing the high-performance management style (White 2021). "Process mapping" is a way of visually representing the flow of work within a department, as well as how that flow relates to the broader flow of work in the organization as a whole. This mapping enables one to perceive the organizational context, as well as highlight the outcomes and purposes of the department and how these relate to the goals of the organization more broadly. This exemplifies a crucial piece of the Deming approach, for the obvious reason that efficiency can only be understood and measured in terms of the goals of the organization: "efficiency" is always an "efficiency for" the sake of some goal, and what might be efficient toward one goal may not be efficient toward another. And finally, the mapping can also highlight areas where the system might be adequate in the abstract, but the training is currently inadequate, thus offering insight into training needs.

APPLYING THE DEMING MODEL

The Deming model and the high-performance management style originally developed primarily in settings of "heavy industry" and only later began to impact organizational theory and practices outside those confines. Nonetheless, the Deming model and approach are useful for other sorts of organizations, including technical services in libraries. TS departments—perhaps more than other departments in most libraries—have undergone substantial changes precisely due to technological shifts, such as those outlined earlier in this chapter (not to mention the accelerated technological changes due to the pandemic). Consequently, TS requires setting up an adequate process of ongoing reflection on inefficiencies in the system that are in need of updating, and consistent training in new technologies.

It is easy to imagine cases of this kind in which this situation applies. Let's suppose a librarian in a university library works in cataloging, but due to both ongoing technological changes in content delivery and exigencies in the shift to electronic resources caused by the pandemic, this librarian runs the risk of having little or no work. Let's further imagine that the library has decided to shift as much as possible to shelf-ready books due to budgetary constraints. In some settings, this team member might be concerned about the loss of their job. Furthermore, if Deming is correct, in many such settings, a person in this position might well recognize certain inefficiencies in the system and might have worthwhile insights about how the system could be improved, but might not bring them up, or even worse, might hide them, precisely out of fear that their job might be lost. This fear would be justified in the case of a (typical) American management system, one in which management evaluates a team member only according to their current usefulness and views them as an expense, rather than an asset.

In contrast, were the Deming approach innate to the library culture in question and if the work of developing the most efficient system for the highest-quality service was understood to be integral to the team member's job, the team member would be a partner in the process of quality control. They would also feel confident that, if the system needed to change, management would do its best to find ways of educating and training the librarian for a new role in the modified system—perhaps by covering roles in the transition to online materials, or working with metadata or gathering usage data.

CONCLUSION

As the preceding example suggests, the Deming approach, though referring first and foremost to a system of management, does not consist solely in such a system. Rather, as Deming himself suggested at various points, the system is in part a product of psychology—both individual and organizational—and rests on a set of attitudes, virtues, and values. Genuine efficiency and effectiveness, in this model, are not a simple sum of the individual parts. They pertain instead to the development of a culture of quality control, in which all team members feel responsible for achieving this goal—in part because they realize that their own contributions are important to improving efficiency, and in part because they can trust that management will not scapegoat individual members or pursue quick profits, but instead aim to help each team member retool as necessary through ongoing training, for the sake of improving the system's functioning and the goal of quality products and services.

Yet this point also underlines one of the central challenges of the Deming model. Though, for example, technical services departments can, as a rule, benefit from the model, there is no guarantee that other library departments or the organization as a whole will seek to improve according to the same model. Library cultures can manifest some inertia when it comes to innovation, based on that aspect of librarianship which seeks to preserve the past. Thus, there can be resistance to models of the Deming variety. The problem of how a department committed to the Deming model functions within an organization that is not committed to the model in an overarching way is an area in need of further research.

REFERENCES

Davis, Jeehyun. 2016. "Transforming Technical Services: Evolving Functions in Large Research University Libraries." *Library Resources & Technical Services* 60, no. 1. https://doi.org/10.5860/lrts.60n1.52.

Deming, W. Edwards. 1986. *Out of the Crisis*. Cambridge: Massachusetts Institute of Technology, Center for Advanced Engineering Study.

Kriemadis, Thanos. 2018. *Ideological Function of Deming Theory in Higher Education: Emerging Research and Opportunities*. Hershey, PA: Information Science Reference.

Laskowski, M. S. and J. A. Maddox Abbot. 2014. "The Evolution of Technical Services: Learning from the Past and Embracing the Future." *Technical Services Quarterly* 31, no. 1: 13–30.

White, K. 2021. "Process Mapping and High Performance Management in Technical Services." In *Technical Services in the 21st Century*, edited by S. S. Hines, 55–67. Advances in Library Administration and Organization, vol. 42. Bingley, UK: Emerald Publishing. https://doi.org/10.1108/S0732-067120210000042006.

White, K., and J. White. 2021. "Accepting Free Content during the COVID-19 Pandemic: An Assessment." *Serials Librarian* 81, no. 1. https://doi.org/10.1080/0361526X.2021.1943106.

4

Just-in-Time Training for Continuous Improvement within a Consortium

Rachel K. Fischer

REGARDLESS OF THE SIZE OF A CONSORTIUM, MAINTAINING THE QUALITY of the records of a shared catalog and continuously training new technical services staff working for multiple libraries can be challenging. Merely providing onboarding training is not enough, given the complexities of the cataloging and acquisitions workflows and the challenges of working in a shared integrated library system (ILS). Whether a staff member forgets to follow a local practice, or an error occurs that could have been avoided by following a documented procedure, no mistake is too small to learn from. Mistakes are not only a learning opportunity for staff, but also an opportunity to identify training needs for an individual library or a whole consortium. Viewing mistakes, questions, and forgotten procedures as an opportunity for continuous improvement will create a supportive organizational culture, improve how staff members learn, and enhance communication.

While hands-on learning in which staff members repeat tasks on the job enables them to become proficient in everyday technical services tasks, it cannot improve recall when a task undertaken is done infrequently, if documentation is lacking, or if documentation cannot be located. Applying lean management concepts such as continuous improvement, or in this case continuous learning, and just-in-time methods can improve the quality of a training program, recall of concepts, communication among consortium members, and the quality of the shared catalog. This chapter explains how pertinent industrial theories that typically improve efficiency can be applied to the training and development of technical services staff. It provides advice and practical suggestions on how continuous improvement techniques can be applied to improve the accessibility and quality of documentation. Real-life examples of issues that have arisen in a public library consortium and how they created a training opportunity demonstrate how just-in-time theories can be included as a training method on the job. Although this chapter is written from the perspective of a consortial training environment, the techniques can easily be applied on a smaller scale. Trainers, managers, and supervisors in charge of training technical services departments in individual libraries can use the advice to improve their training techniques and intradepartmental communication in the same manner that a consortium would.

LEAN MANAGEMENT THEORIES AS APPLIED TO TRAINING

The concept of lean management comprises numerous management techniques that strive to do more with less by eliminating waste, or muda in Japanese, from the production process. The seven types of waste are inventory, waiting time, defects, overproduction, excess movement, transportation, and over-processing. Some of the management techniques under the lean management umbrella include just-in-time and Kaizen, which means "continuous improvement" in Japanese. Toyota, the company that popularized lean management techniques, idealizes lean management as a vision of "striving for perfection while recognizing there is no perfect process" (Liker and Ross 2017, xxi). Perfectionism, efficiency, cooperation, and cost-saving methods are not unfamiliar to library technical service departments. Lean management and continuous improvement techniques have already been used by libraries to analyze and improve their workflows for the purpose of operational excellence.

Striving for perfection, even while recognizing that nothing is perfect, does not create a supportive atmosphere, but one that lacks acceptance for mistakes. Masaaki Imai, the founder of the Kaizen Institute, advocates for a different viewpoint. He views continuous improvement as a commonsense approach that is integral to a successful business strategy (Imai 2012). Viewing continuous improvement in this way is a more realistic mindset because commonsense behaviors can be internalized and repeated on the job.

The creative processes necessary for crafting a training and development program for a whole consortium or an individual library may seem like a minor part of the daily workflow of an individual library's technical services department. However, production-based departments can become more efficient when training courses and materials are easily accessible, can be referred to while on the job, used as a guide while learning tasks, and accommodate multiple learning styles and abilities, and are improved as needed. Trainers don't need to be experts on every technique that falls under the lean management umbrella, nor do they need to be experts on the Kaizen style of assessing workflow efficiency. However, internalizing some commonsense aspects of the continuous improvement and just-in-time philosophies can make a big difference to the members of a consortium or an individual library.

CONTINUOUS IMPROVEMENT

Continuous improvement, or Kaizen, is the concept that employees should work together to incrementally improve the processes and quality of the organization. A commonsense example of how this can become part of an organization's culture is through an evaluation process. A trainer can ask staff to beta-test a new training program and then offer suggestions on how to improve that program, or the trainer can use surveys to assess a training program or webinar after the training has occurred. The trainer should immediately update the training program with the suggestions, or plan on adding new documentation, webinars, or courses. Some libraries have a simple suggestion box to accept suggestions throughout the year. A consortium or individual library can do so electronically by announcing that suggestions can be sent to the help desk or a specific e-mail address, or by filling out a survey.

Adopting the mindset that any comments submitted via discussion lists or the help desk's ticketing system could provide an idea to improve training is an important step in internalizing continuous improvement. These comments could come in the form of an e-mail pointing out an error in a document, a question about documentation that cannot be found, a request for assistance on improving the workflow, or in the course of helping technical services staff with technical problems. Calling attention to mistakes or holes in the training documentation and correcting them can prevent the technical services staff from making future mistakes. This process of mistake-proofing is called poke yoke in Japanese. For technical services staff, this could look like adding regular reminders of processes and procedures to meetings without judging those who made mistakes. As previously mentioned, trainers can ask other staff to review the training material to identify mistakes in it before training employees. Correcting mistakes and improving training as quickly as possible will prevent the technical services staff from making future mistakes, eliminate time that would otherwise have been wasted, and improve the department's efficiency.

Another commonsense continuous improvement practice is good housekeeping, or 5S. Five S stands for sort, straighten, scrub, systematize, and standardize. Masaaki Imai has stated: "As a general rule of thumb, introducing good housekeeping in the gemba [workplace] reduces the failure rate by 50 percent, and standardization further reduces the failure rate by 50 percent of the new figure" (Imai 2012, xvi). For many workplaces, this means keeping the office or manufacturing equipment clean and standardizing the procedures. For trainers, this means assessing the documentation, videos, and courses to make them easily accessible and standardized. Instead of having one document for a manual, having separate documents or web pages for each topic that can be easily searched and printed out makes training more efficient for new employees as they learn to use new software or a new workflow. Without a second screen, printouts are a necessity when an employee needs to follow the steps to learn new software or procedures in an accelerated manner. Adding as many screenshots as possible to documentation is important to accelerate the learning process. Without screenshots, it can be difficult for visual learners to identify the correct icon or remember which drop-down menu contains which functionality. Supplementing documents with short videos that document one process at a time is important for visualizing and internalizing how software functions. Keeping videos and documents to a manageable length (under ten minutes) or focused on just one process makes it easier for employees to refer to them as needed.

MICROLEARNING AND JUST-IN-TIME TRAINING

The concept of creating training materials in shorter, focused chunks is known by e-learning professionals as "microlearning." While microlearning has been lauded for its compatibility with web-based, mobile learning, it can also be applicable to shorter documents or brief presentations at meetings. After a concept is introduced at a meeting and questions have been addressed, the concept can be repeated as a microlearning video with a handout and included on a website. The accessibility of shorter and more focused documentation or videos helps to reinforce concepts while on the job as an aid to completing a task, or as a quick refresher between tasks. These episodic lessons can be organized on websites according to competency to support competency training programs or used on an as-needed basis to support a just-in-time training strategy (Emerson and Berge 2018).

Just-in-time is a management strategy that is typically applied to manufacturing. For example, print-on-demand books are not printed until an order for a print book has been placed. Creating a whole training program around the idea of just-in-time training is unrealistic, but the strategy can be used to supplement a training and development program to improve documentation and provide training in small amounts when it is needed. Thus, just-in-time training can be used as a continuous improvement technique. By continually evaluating the training needs of library staff through the assessment methods previously mentioned, the just-in-time principle can be applied to learning and development by providing training on a continual basis throughout the year when it is needed. This can be done by monitoring help desk tickets or e-mails for questions on topics that are not addressed in existing documentation. If one staff member has a question, everyone could benefit from a refresher on the topic. The documentation is then updated immediately. Training and development staff can provide training in the style of microlearning as brief documents, videos, or training sessions when it is needed. In so doing, the concept of just-in-time training occurs naturally with the assessment process.

CONTINUOUS LEARNING SCENARIOS

The member services librarians for Cooperative Computer Services (CCS), a consortium of public libraries in Illinois, train the members' library staff to use the library management system, provide technical support for the ILS, and offer consulting services to the member libraries. On a regular basis, the member services librarian for the consortium's technical services departments encounters questions from technical services staff, and some of these offer good "just-in-time" training opportunities. To apply the just-in-time and continuous improvement principles to a training program, it is important that the technical services staff feel comfortable asking questions and making suggestions.

Having multiple outlets for these questions can provide a trainer with ideas of when additional documentation or live training is needed. The consortium staff at CCS monitor multiple communication channels to identify topics they can present on as training components during meetings, webinars, training courses, or to incorporate in new documentation. These channels include:

- An e-mail discussion list that allows member library staff to ask each other questions about policies, procedures, and workflows
- A help desk ticketing system that allows member library staff to report errors in the catalog and ask questions about cataloging practices, cataloging workflows, or acquisitions workflows
- Motions passed at governance meetings that lead to changes in cataloging practices or changes to cataloging or acquisitions workflows
- Surveys of webinar and course attendees to assess the quality of the program and determine future training needs
- The announcements of new developments that have occurred in national cataloging standards
- The announcement of software upgrades to the ILS

Help desk ticketing systems have tagging systems built in to help users categorize issues. Trainers can keep track of potential training opportunities by adding a tag to the ticket. If help desk software is too expensive for a consortium or individual library, a form can be added to a website that sends an e-mail to a centralized e-mail address. E-mails can be categorized or placed in folders to keep track of training-related questions. While the member services librarians at CCS try to immediately update documentation when errors need correcting or more details need to be included, they also make lists to keep track of training opportunities that can be included as a short refresher during a meeting or that need to be turned into a video or webinar.

Here are several real-life scenarios of questions that technical services staff have posed, the training opportunity that proceeded from the question, and the continuous improvement effort that ensued.

Scenario 1: Avoiding Duplicate Records

A cataloging librarian reported to the help desk that an error occurred when loading records to the catalog from OCLC Connexion. Upon examination, the member services librarian discovered that the cataloging librarian had exported duplicate records from Connexion. The member services librarian responded with an explanation and tips for using Connexion to ensure this would not happen again. Several months later, a cataloging librarian from a different library reported the same problem. After providing tips on how to prevent this from happening, the member services librarian made note of the training opportunity.

Before the next meeting of catalogers from all member libraries, the member services librarian created a document that provided tips on avoiding exporting duplicates from OCLC Connexion, and she added a link to the document on a procedural page of a website. At the next meeting for catalogers of all the libraries, the member services librarian provided a live demonstration on the cause of this problem, and ways to export records from OCLC Connexion that would prevent duplicates from being exported. If this had not been viewed as a training opportunity, catalogers would have continued to report this problem to the help desk. Creating documentation and presenting on this topic occurred "just in time" to prevent future problems. After identifying a training opportunity, the creation of documentation contributed to the continuous improvement of the consortium by preventing future errors from occurring at the member libraries and reducing the number of future help-desk tickets, since all catalogers in the consortium could now solve this problem on their own.

Scenario 2: Organizing Documentation

It is normal for the procedures of infrequently completed tasks to be forgotten. A certain amount of repetition is required to memorize procedures. Catalogers encounter serials title changes or special issues so infrequently that when they encounter a title change or special issue, they like to write to the help desk to confirm that they understand the procedures and follow the local practice properly. It can also be easy to forget where this documentation is located because it is on multiple websites. The member services librarian responded to these questions by sending catalogers the links to the pages containing the procedures and local cataloging practices.

Like the previous scenario, multiple catalogers had the same question on these special cataloging issues over a period of several months. When this happens, the member services librarian likes to think of it as an opportunity for improvement. When she examined the documentation, it seemed disorganized. Separate information on the same topic was located on two separate pages, in addition to catalogers needing to refer to the CONSER manual on an external website. The member services librarian added this topic to the list of documentation that should be reviewed and consolidated onto one web page. However, the librarian would need to consult with the advisory group in charge of the cataloging manual before taking an opportunity for 5S on the topic. Although a demonstration on the topic at a meeting was unnecessary, including a brief reminder of the location of the procedural pages and CONSER's policy on special issues will allow catalogers to review the procedures on their own time as a microlearning opportunity.

Scenario 3: Training Acquisitions Staff on Bulk Changes

An acquisitions librarian created a help desk ticket because the automated processes that create item records when purchase orders are released did not choose the correct item record templates, and so erroneous data appeared in the "on-order" item records. After discussing the problem with the librarian and examining the records, it was clear that there were too many item templates for the automated process to work without placing the name of the template in a specific field in the bibliographic record. The member services librarian suggested that they could add a step to their workflow that adds the necessary field to their bibliographic records, using the bibliographic bulk change feature of the catalog when this field is not added to records. Bibliographic bulk changes are usually completed by catalogers, not acquisitions staff. So, the acquisitions librarian did not have a lot of experience with this task. The member services librarian sent the acquisitions librarian instructions with screenshots and a sample bibliographic record to look at.

Since this topic is unfamiliar to acquisitions, it warranted planning for a microlearning opportunity and a full webinar. The member services librarian created a document with step-by-step instructions and demonstrated this one task at a meeting. Having become aware (through a recent survey) that others desired more bulk change training, the librarian knew that planning a webinar on all bulk change features for the benefit of both catalogers and acquisitions staff would provide the member libraries with the ability to improve their own workflows while also improving the quality of the consortium's training program.

CONCLUSION

While perfection is not possible, always striving to improve demonstrates strong leadership, respect, accessibility, and inclusion while supporting the mission of a library consortium or individual library. Internalizing the assessment and planning processes that support a continuous improvement training strategy will benefit the consortium by providing the excellent quality of service that member libraries need to improve their own departments and workflows. Trainers, managers, or supervisors at individual libraries can apply this to their own technical services departments by assessing their own training methods to support continuous improvement within the department. This can be done by listening to the needs of the members or department staff, adjusting documentation and training courses quickly, and then providing microlearning opportunities where training is needed the most. Efficient and well-crafted training and development programs can help technical services departments eliminate wasted time by accelerating learning and eliminating mistakes before they occur.

REFERENCES

Emerson, L. C., and Z. L. Berge. 2018. "Microlearning: Knowledge Management Applications and Competency-Based Training in the Workplace." *Knowledge Management & E-Learning* 10, no. 2: 125–32.

Fox, Amy. 2016. "Microlearning for Effective Performance Management." *TD: Talent Development* 70, no. 4: 116–17.

Imai, Masaaki. 2012. *Gemba Kaizen: A Commonsense Approach to a Continuous Improvement Strategy.* New York: McGraw Hill.

Liker, Jeffrey K., and Karyn Ross. 2017. *The Toyota Way to Service Excellence: Lean Transformation in Service Organizations.* New York: McGraw Hill Education.

5

Practicing Partnerships

A Case Study on How Realizing an In-House Cataloging Course Set the Stage for a Collaborative Future

Juliya Borie, May Chan, Elisa Sze, and Polina Vendrova

IN THE FALL OF 2019, THE METADATA SERVICES DEPARTMENT AT THE UNIversity of Toronto Libraries (UTL) piloted an in-house introductory cataloging course targeting a diverse group of staff from three technical services departments, including librarians, senior and junior technicians, clerical staff, and student employees. The course was designed to demystify cataloging theory and practice to staff members who supported the work through narrow routines and tasks. It was also designed to encourage flexible, collaborative ways of working. The timing and context of the course were complicated by the fact that all three of the departments involved (Metadata Services, Acquisitions, and Metadata Technologies) were being impacted by continual staffing changes, and that UTL was at the beginning stages of migrating to a new library services platform (LSP).

Timing and context thus shaped the instructional design, execution, and outcomes of the course. When planning, the authors took care to balance service demands, flux in staffing in a complex labor environment, and staff development pending a system migration. This migration unexpectedly took place during the COVID-19 pandemic, requiring staff to adapt to remote work. The in-house course was instrumental in preparing staff to navigate this unexpected change.

While the context in which the course was delivered is specific to UTL, themes of relationship-building, peer leadership, and developing a culture of continual learning will be of interest to technical services managers, coordinators of staff training programs, and trainers everywhere. This case study integrates the perspectives of its four authors, each of whom also played a significant role in the LSP transition.

SITUATING THIS CASE STUDY IN THE BROADER LIS LITERATURE

Training has been a theme found in LIS literature over the decades. Stites notes that the impetus behind training often includes helping staff develop a new mindset toward their work, enhancing staff performance, rewarding staff, building team cohesion, complying with regulations and certification, or changing "organizational outcomes" (2009, 240). The need to shape staff members' mindsets, build team cohesion, and change organizational outcomes influenced the conception of the Metadata Services in-house course.

The literature has traditionally presented cataloging training as an activity customized to particular staff members' knowledge, skills, and experience. By contrast, departmental programs designed to reach multiple levels and types of staff roles simultaneously—like the Metadata Services in-house course—are discussed only infrequently. In a special themed issue of *Cataloging and Classification Quarterly* from August 1987, Hudson expresses the prevailing thinking on training at the time: its purpose is to increase the work outputs of a team, and train catalogers to "produce error-free cataloging records at reasonable levels of production" (1987, 77). Although cataloging training programs tend to follow a pattern, they are challenging to standardize because every staff member arrives with different experiences and their own speed of learning (Hudson 1987, 70).

The case studies in the literature vary in their focus, from the need to train staff on new cataloging standards or automated systems, to cross-training staff from other functional areas—but all such studies recognize that training programs are expensive in terms of staff time. Gelber and Kandarasheva discuss Columbia University Library's program to train copy catalogers in PCC and NACO principles, though they acknowledge that labor considerations might limit the applicability of Columbia's experience to other libraries (2011). Similarly, Morris and Wiggins discuss the intensive 36-hour training program the Library of Congress organized for its catalogers and reference librarians on the original RDA (2016).

Articles discussing the assessment of staff cataloging skills raise a perennial question: who should be responsible for cataloging training: LIS schools, or employers? Gorman's view—that teaching LIS students to catalog helps them to "understand the way in which recorded knowledge and information is organized for retrieval"—has long held its place in LIS curriculum development (Gorman 1997). However, the unionized staff at UTL don't necessarily have any formal library school education, either through an ALA-accredited program or library technician certification. Moreover, the library profession remains divided on how trainers should balance theory and practice. As Snow and Hoffmann (2015) state, it is nearly impossible to settle on a universally "ideal" ratio: although the most effective cataloging courses in LIS schools tend to offer both theory and practice, many professionals differ on what comprises theory. Furthermore, training must be provided within a real-world context (Snow and Hoffman 2015). The structure of the Metadata Services in-house course emphasized on-the-job application, reinforced through assigned exercises, drop-in clinics before class, and weekly tutorials.

The value that librarians and library workers place on on-the-job training is evident beyond the North American context. In Israel, instructors develop course materials in the expectation that novice catalogers will later round out their knowledge on the job (Shoham 2006, 458). Kwak's survey of cataloging librarians across ninety-eight universities in South Korea revealed unanimous agreement among respondents that cataloging professionals need job training; moreover, employers should provide financial and administrative support for job training programs and individual self-training (2005).

CONTEXT AT UTL

At UTL, training has traditionally happened on the job. While professional development is encouraged for all UTL staff, access to it has been uneven among different employee groups there. As members of the faculty association, bound by policies around professional practice, librarians with at least a 25 percent full-time-equivalent appointment have access to a professional expense reimbursement allowance to cover the costs of their professional development activities. Unionized staff do not have this allowance because professional development and performance assessments are not written into their appointments.

Additionally, training was inconsistent among the UTL staff. Cross-training tended to be reactive, rather than proactive. Some supervisors assigned specific tasks to individuals on the same team for short-term efficiency instead of cross-training for long-term sustainability. Training for unionized employees did not always provide context or theory, which limited both their understanding of the impact of their work on other parts of the workflow and their own problem-solving capacity. Documentation for workflows and standard practices was customized to individual staff roles, paper-based, and not readily accessible. Prior to the in-house course, some staff took external courses out of interest; however, there was no follow-up or clear on-the-job application.

Another challenge was the numerous staffing changes that took place between 2017 and 2019 in the three technical departments, including various departures and arrivals and a restructuring of roles. Particularly notable was the replacement of dedicated copy catalogers with junior technicians shared with the Acquisitions Department to process 80,000 new titles annually.

These staffing changes also occurred during a time when personnel who were well positioned to introduce new ways of thinking, such as unit heads and supervisors, were in flux, creating an environment with unclear priorities. Some supervisors and managers had set ideas of what cataloging work involved. Constant changes in these roles resulted in tensions on how to employ the new shared positions. Uneven access to training resulted in inequitable development. Developing single experts led to knowledge and service gaps when they went on leave, were seconded, or found jobs elsewhere.

COURSE INSTRUCTORS AND TUTORS

While the authors of this chapter come from diverse backgrounds and play distinct roles in Metadata Services, they all have teaching experience and enjoy teaching. They also share a vision of fostering a collaborative culture within and beyond their own department, increasing the visibility of cataloging, promoting partnerships with other units, and demystifying cataloging work as much as possible. The in-house course was a proactive effort to create a more collaborative and inclusive learning environment for all technical services units amidst change and uncertainty. Juliya and May served as the course instructors, while Elisa and Polina served as course tutors. The instructors decided on and delivered course content in consultation with the tutors, and the tutors provided in-class support and facilitated pre-class clinics. Both instructors and tutors also led tutorial groups outside of class.

COURSE PLANNING

The goals for the three-month course included imparting a baseline knowledge of cataloging theory and practices, encouraging team cohesion among staff shared between departments, defining and assigning appropriate levels of cataloging complexity to staff members, and reducing the barriers to development opportunities for unionized staff in a traditional learning culture focused on librarians. Overall, the instructors wanted the course to reduce misunderstanding about what cataloging work entails as well as provide an overview of the cataloging standards and utilities that support copy cataloging workflows. In planning the course, Juliya and May, as the instructors, factored in:

- Cataloging knowledge related to various parts of the technical services workflow
- The need to distinguish between original, derived, and copy cataloging
- Labor considerations

Given that the instructors, tutors, and participants were from four different employee groups, the instructors consulted with Human Resources on how to offer the course without creating the impression of asking staff to do more than their positions require.

Bloom's *Taxonomy of Educational Objectives* (1956) was one framework used for developing the course's educational goals, objectives, curriculum, and learning experiences. Because the course was introductory in nature, the exercises and activities were kept to the knowledge and understanding levels of cognitive learning, as outlined by Bloom. After students had been introduced to concepts and standards in the first three sessions, they were given opportunities to apply them in increasingly complex ways.

To build on the students' newly acquired knowledge and skills, course planners adopted Vygotsky's scaffolded approach, which emphasizes the importance of social interaction for learning (Vygotsky 1978). To get participants to practice cataloging tasks with social support, tutorial groups that would meet outside of class time were created and assigned to an instructor or tutor. In addition to the two-hour weekly sessions and small-group tutorials, informal drop-in clinics were set up before class in which participants and tutors could work on cataloging examples and questions. These features of the course recognized the various positions, experience, and levels of responsibility of participants, while allowing customized learning for those with similar backgrounds as well as promoting peer engagement. The course syllabus drew upon and adapted materials from INF2145, a Faculty of Information course taught by Elisa at the University of Toronto; and LIBR511, a School of Information course co-taught by May and Maryann Kempthorne at the University of British Columbia. See figure 5.1 for the course outline.

EXECUTION AND TEACHING

Over nine sessions, the course covered core cataloging standards, some utilities used to support copy cataloging, Metadata Services workflows, and their connections with acquisitions work. The course was not intended to replace individualized training for copy cataloging tasks and workflows, nor did the authors expect participants to become proficient at copy cataloging by the last session. Nonetheless, it was important to ensure that each class included both theoretical and hands-on components; those already performing copy cataloging would benefit from learning the foundational theory behind their practices, and those not doing this work would gain practice and learn to recognize the decision-making involved. For these reasons, each class took place in a computer lab, where everyone had their own workstation and could access the bibliographic utilities needed.

To build a respectful and inclusive classroom environment, session 1 included a small-group discussion to jointly develop learning guidelines with the participants. Participants responding to the question "What does a positive learning environment look like?" highlighted the importance of open lines of communication for successful learning.

The first hour of each session consisted of a lecture on the principles and theories underlying a particular practice. After a break, the second hour was devoted to practical activities. In one class, participants searched for records using bibliographic tools such as iSearch (developed in-house for batch ISBN searches), SmartPort (a Z39.50 utility built into the integrated library system used at the time), and OCLC Connexion. In another class, participants were

FIGURE 5.1
Course outline

COURSE STRUCTURE	
Session #	**Session components**
1. Course Overview; Introduction to Standards	• Overview of approach, course goals and objectives, quizzes and assignments • Participation and learning guidelines (group activity) • Presentation: Introduction to cataloging standards • Quiz: Demystifying acronyms • Assignment: Navigate and create a toolbox including bookmarks for various standards (RDA, MARC 21, LCSH, LCC, DDC, ISBD)
2. RDA	• Presentation: RDA—an overview • Quiz: RDA for copy cataloging • Assignment: Describe one notable change in RDA and how this change would impact access for the user.
3. MARC21 Bibliographic	• Presentation: MARC21 Bibliographic • MARC 21 Basics quiz and MARC 21 Bibliographic assignment (questions on components of a sample MARC record)
4. Putting RDA and MARC Together	• Quiz on RDA Terminology • Presentation: RDA in MARC 21, Identifying RDA records • Assignment to assess records based on supplied criteria
5. Authorities	• Presentation: Authorities • Quiz on authority records
6. Classification and Shelf-listing	• Presentation: Classification • Exercises on classification • Presentation: Shelflisting
7. Local Practices and Workflows	• Presentation: Workflows • Technical services workflow group exercise
8. Identifying Resource Types; Holdings Work	• Presentation: Resource types • Exercise: Identify sample resources and indicate whether the resources are monographic series or serials or continuations.
9. Development Paths	• Presentation: Development paths; core competencies; development opportunities • Course evaluation

asked to check assigned item call numbers against the shelflist. In the class on differences between serials, monographic series, and multivolume monographic sets, physical copies from the department's backlog were circulated so that participants could see the complex range of these publication types, and appreciate the different data elements that potentially need to be recorded in bibliographic descriptions. The hands-on activities yielded questions and discussions that were useful for fine-tuning future sessions; if a particular exercise generated many questions, the instructors addressed them the following week.

For the instructors and tutors, Microsoft Teams became a useful tool for the collaborative review of slides and other course materials. Finalized course materials were published on Quercus, the university's iteration of the Canvas course management system. The instructors posted slides in advance, enabling participants to download them or follow along during class. Each discrete topic or exercise received its own page in the Quercus weekly module. The instructors borrowed a teaching technique from the Carpentries community by setting up a weekly whiteboard for collaborative note-taking (Carpentries 2021). These virtual whiteboards were openly editable Google Documents that were updated in real time and were accessible from a secure link shared with the class. Finally, multiple modules contained at least one quiz or homework assignment for participants to complete by the next class. The supervisors made sure that participants had work time to complete these modules. Most quizzes were designed to be auto-graded. In order to evaluate the participants' work on the assignments, the instructor released solutions at the start of the following class and addressed general questions. Tutors were tasked with scheduling tutorials with their cluster of participants so they could discuss solutions in depth.

In addition to the tutorials, drop-in clinics were scheduled in the hour before class. During these clinics, participants could ask questions about content previously covered, or stemming from individual exploration of a topic. Tutors used the clinics to strengthen the sense that cataloging expertise was spread across the department, rather than belonging to a few individuals. To encourage new relationships, participants were invited to connect with any of the tutors, not just with the one assigned to them. Participants could interact with each other in a casual environment, especially when one tutor was working with two or more participants simultaneously. The opportunity for participants to work through the same issues together built a sense of collegiality among them.

OUTCOMES OF THE PILOT COURSE

As the authors had hoped, the course strengthened team cohesion and staff members' respect for different roles across technical services. Throughout the course, the instructors and tutors observed that participants were curious about their coworkers' roles and responsibilities. In the post-course survey, respondents cited conversations between staff members which suggested that the participants enjoyed learning alongside their peers, and felt more comfortable asking for help because they now shared a common knowledge base. One participant valued the partnerships created, explaining that the course helped with seeing technical services in context and setting career goals. These outcomes were especially welcome because past departmental surveys had indicated a desire for better communication across reporting lines.

Unexpectedly, aside from positioning the team well for future cross-training, the strengthening of work relationships happened at an opportune time: three months after the course concluded, the COVID-19 pandemic required a shift to remote work just as UTL was beginning a challenging migration from an integrated library system to a cloud-based LSP environment. The trust generated among the department's staff and their familiarity with cloud-based educational and collaborative work tools made it easier for many to navigate this change.

For instance, to assist with the LSP transition for catalogers across the complex, tri-campus library system, all four authors joined the Metadata Management Functional Team and contributed to planning and delivering LSP staff training. Their experience as course instructors and tutors prepared them for the facilitation and training skills needed during a global pandemic, and helped to bolster the feeling of trust essential for strengthening relationships and adapting work to difficult and mutable circumstances. The authors' familiarity with online teaching tools further eased their sudden transition to a remote environment. UTL chose Quercus as the tool for rolling out LSP training, a platform that instructors, tutors, and learners were already familiar with from the course. Finally, Microsoft Teams became a critical platform for day-to-day communications and file-sharing across UTL during the pandemic.

Through a coincidence of timing, the planning and delivery of the departmental course helped the staff to continue performing critical work at a challenging time.

CONCLUSION

Delivering an in-house course on cataloging is an undertaking that requires significant resources. In this case, a unique confluence of staffing changes, staff needs, and collective instructional experience enabled the authors to run this pilot.

The decision to develop a course for staff with varying backgrounds and jobs—some of which did not include cataloging tasks—might be considered ambitious and risky. Some post-course survey responses indicated that too much material had been covered; and some participants wanted more time spent on each topic. However, the positive outcomes of the pilot led the authors to conclude that strengthening collegial respect and appreciation for the labor involved in cataloging work was worth the investment of time and energy. The course helped build a collaborative team mentality, tapped into the intellectual curiosity and engagement of staff who had previously viewed their work as a mere sequence of tasks, and developed a supportive environment that encourages continual learning. These long-term benefits have helped the department remain agile and productive in uncertain times.

One-on-one training between supervisors and staff remains an important component of skills development, especially in cataloging work. Nonetheless, the authors see a role for departmental courses that bring together team members in varying roles. If the authors were to run a second iteration of this course—for instance, to target new hires who have since joined technical services or to cross-train public services staff—some modifications to consider include adjusting the balance of theory versus practice, building in more hands-on learning, and situating catalogers' decision-making more firmly in the concept of "user tasks."

Lastly, this course would not have been realized without the support of senior staff and supervisors, the willingness of instructors and tutors to assist in developing and delivering the course, and the enthusiastic commitment of the participants who took a chance on the pilot.

REFERENCES

Bloom, Benjamin S. 1956. *Taxonomy of Educational Objectives: The Classification of Educational Goals.* New York: D. McKay.

The Carpentries. 2021. "Instructor Training." https://carpentries.github.io/instructor-training/.

Gelber, Natalia, and Irina Kandarasheva. 2011. "PCC Training for Copy Catalogers: Is It Worth the Investment? The Columbia University Libraries Experience." *Library Resources & Technical Services* 55, no. 3: 163–71.

Gorman, Michael. 1997. "What Is the Future of Cataloguing and Cataloguers?" Presentation at 63rd IFLA General Conference. http://archive.ifla.org/IV/ifla63/63gorm.htm.

Hudson, Judith. 1987. "On-the-Job Training for Cataloging and Classification." *Cataloging & Classification Quarterly* 7, no. 4: 69–78. https://doi.org/10.1300/J104v07n04_06.

Kwak, Chul-Wan. 2005. "A Study of On the Job Training and Self-Training of the Cataloging and Classification Librarians Working in South Korean Academic Libraries." *Cataloging & Classification Quarterly* 41, no. 2: 135–47. https://doi.org/10.1300/J104v41n02_09.

Morris, Susan R., and Beacher Wiggins. 2016. "Implementing RDA at the Library of Congress." *JLIS.It* 7, no. 2: 199–228.

Shoham, Snunith. 2006. "Cataloging Instruction in Israel." *Cataloging & Classification Quarterly* 41, no. 3–4: 443–60. https://doi.org/10.1300/J104v41n03_13.

Snow, Karen, and Gretchen L. Hoffman. 2015. "What Makes an Effective Cataloging Course? A Study of the Factors That Promote Learning." *Library Resources & Technical Services* 59, no. 4: 187–99. https://doi.org/10.5860/lrts.59n4.187.

Stites, Barbara J. 2009. "An Unrelenting Need for Training." *Advances in Library Administration and Organization* 28:219–82. Bingley, UK: Emerald Group Publishing.

Vygotsky, L. S. 1978. *Mind in Society: The Development of Higher Psychological Processes.* Cambridge, MA: Harvard University Press.

6

Cross-Organizational Learning through a Community of Practice

Laura Sill

THIS CHAPTER EXPLORES A CASE STUDY FROM THE HESBURGH LIBRARIES of the University of Notre Dame in which fostering a learning organization through the use of a "community of practice" facilitated cross-organizational understanding of metadata asset management within the libraries. Several significant organizational changes at the Hesburgh Libraries since 2011, including staff retirements, organizational redesign, pandemic management, and increased awareness of the value of the organizational management of metadata, had prompted the need to think differently about meeting the organization's goals and providing learning for those who create and consume metadata within the libraries.

BACKGROUND

Hesburgh Libraries has reorganized several times (Hesburgh Libraries, n.d., 2016, 2020), prompted twice by a university-sponsored staff retirement incentive program, which significantly reshaped the size and makeup of metadata and cataloging services throughout the libraries. Those staff who remained on board with skills in this area applied their knowledge and expertise to a broader range of schema and encoding practices to accommodate new systems and means of delivery. The libraries' collections had expanded in format and type to reflect a greater emphasis on digital collections and e-preferred collecting models and services. The existing distribution of metadata respon-sibilities across the organization to various collection-processing and service operations, however, did not facilitate the consistent creation and manage-ment of collection metadata across the new systems. Metadata and cataloging staff held valuable local practice documentation in closed file repositories or, worse yet, shared their practices verbally between one another in the unit. Skills development fell to unit managers on an as-needed basis, and training across unit lines was less than consistently carried out. Moreover, as new sys-tems or services development projects launched, the impact that metadata would play on these efforts was not an up-front consideration.

In 2018, the Hesburgh Libraries published a report called "Defining a Trans-formative Research Library for the University of Notre Dame," which high-lighted staff learning and growth as a key value, and called for assurances that "time for learning is visible" (Hesburgh Libraries 2018, 22). Over the course of the ensuing transformation, it was found that processes, services, and decision-making were most successful in those domain areas where cross-sector relationships were strong. In the distributed metadata management area, however, these relationships were not strong. A new, adaptable learn-ing culture was needed so that "honesty, openness, questioning, listening, and sharing" would be possible across unit lines. The metadata area's culture needed to support the voices of all metadata traditions and be one that made "defensiveness discussable" (Phipps 1993). By 2020, the Hesburgh Libraries had charged a newly created Metadata Services program with developing a strategy that would work toward a consistent and cohesive approach to meta-data work and development.

COMMUNITY OF PRACTICE AS A FRAMEWORK TO SUPPORT LEARNING

Framing and nurturing a learning environment became a central focus for the Metadata Services program and specifically for its program director, who chose to explore a "community of practice" as a way to mobilize and connect metadata creators, curators, and consumers. The program also called for hav-ing a shared organizational purpose in order to strengthen the overall health of resource metadata assets and bring transparency to the organization's metadata practices.

Etienne Wenger introduced the concept of a "community of practice" in his seminal work *Communities of Practice: Learning, Meaning and Identity* (1998). The concept's key components are present in its name: community, implying a gathering of individuals, and a social construct or place for learning; and practice, implying having firsthand knowledge of something and experience to share. Less clear from this name is the component of "domain," or the identity that the community creates and shares over time, and that if nurtured well, fuels a further desire to collaborate around practice (Wenger 1998).

Above all, a community of practice emphasizes learning in a social context. This model provided a way for the Hesburgh Libraries to bring metadata practitioners together in a learning setting where there was a respectful acknowledgment of similarities and differences, which in turn served as the basis for learning from each other and for expanding capacity to address organizational issues that had once been addressed exclusively within operational confines. Because metadata work takes place in information systems and it directly affects discovery and delivery services, the community of practice also provided a way for the Hesburgh Libraries' information technology, user experience, and research services operations to be equal players in the learning process. According to Wenger, "Socially defined competence is always in interplay with our experience. It is in this interplay that learning takes place" (2000, 226). Wenger also cautions that communities of practice "are the cradles of the human spirit, but they can also be its cages" (230). The formation of the Hesburgh Libraries' Metadata Community of Practice (MCoP) required leadership and a commitment to creating learning opportunities that encouraged an open, flexible, and agnostic view of metadata work.

THE HESBURGH LIBRARIES' METADATA COMMUNITY OF PRACTICE

To explore the formation of a community of practice, the Metadata Services program director first identified the community's stakeholders, as described by Wenger (1998, 119). The stakeholders, which included creators (catalogers, metadata and archival practitioners) and consumers (user experience, digitization, and web specialists), met to discuss problems in the metadata domain and to consider how a community of practice might assist. Gauging interest and exploring options with a broad stakeholder group proved to be a positive and critical step in establishing the new learning community. Understanding the problems to be solved from a wide range of perspectives established the stakeholders' commitment to each other and helped them to identify local biases about cataloging work that had hampered progress in recent years. The design of the new group reflected the consensus and expectations of the stakeholders. (See figure 6.1.) At the center of the model is community sponsorship and management, carried out by the MCoP Governance Squad, which focuses on the care and development of learning within the community. Surrounding the center are areas that define the domain as set by stakeholders. Closely related and forming yet another ring around the domain areas are the measures of success or outcomes of the MCoP; and finally, to either side, are listings of stakeholders who define and challenge the development of the community over time.

CULTIVATING A LEARNING ORGANIZATION THROUGH THE MCOP

Programming for the new community considered learning outcomes, learning methods, and learning assessment for each gathering. With systemic problems to solve, the MCoP had to be more than a discussion group. It needed to ensure an interplay of social experience and expertise. Those most impacted by each topic or issue were identified and invited directly to participate in the community's sessions, along with open invitations for participation by all library staff. The goal was to share, educate, and consider the broader impact, actions, and direction around each topic that was considered.

The community of practice became the administrative apparatus in which a learning organization could develop at Hesburgh Libraries. There are various ways to define a "learning organization" (Jain and Mutula 2008). This case study uses Marquardt's definition from his chapter in *The Oxford Handbook of the Learning Organization*: a learning organization is one "that continuously learns, adapts, and improves; and is able to systematically connect the improved learning to the planning and achieving of organizational goals" (2020, 106).

FIGURE 6.1
MCoP concept map

Key:
1. Sponsors who nurture the learning community
2. Domain area / identity definition
3. Activities that signal measures of success
4. Core & boundary stakeholders

To be successful, an organization and its people, technology, and knowledge subsystems must overlap with what becomes the learning system. For example, a community of practice has a people subsystem, with its members forming "part of the learning chain" (Marquardt 2020, 107). The MCoP invited all interested library staff to take part in the learning process and to be free to raise issues, share expertise, and work toward a common understanding and level of competency in the metadata domain. Sarder characterizes a learning system as a deliberate effort to transform an organization by understanding the outcomes one wishes to see and using effective methods for delivering those outcomes, assessing growth, and driving the further development of a learning program (Sarder 2016, 16–19).

HOW MCOP SUPPORTS LEARNING

As the MCoP Governance Squad planned each MCoP meeting, it ensured that three aspects were in place:

1. *Learning outcomes or deliverables.* This expectation includes a clear statement of what the session will teach or provide the participants; that is, what will members get out of the session that will further their understanding or thinking. The meeting invitations specify the anticipated outcome, so library staff can decide whether they wish to participate and they can understand how the discussion might influence their work or professional development.

2. *Learning methods.* These activities, techniques, or approaches deliver content and create a meaningful learning experience for members. With the MCoP forming during the COVID-19 pandemic, all its meetings have been virtual or online to the present, which influenced the methods used.

3. *Learning assessment.* This important step gathers participants' feedback and determines the success of the intended outcome. This process was mostly carried out through online Google Forms surveys, which were sent immediately after each session, although other techniques, such as in-session quizzes, were also utilized.

The MCoP Governance Squad's communication, documentation, and data gathering included all three of these learning aspects. The following two examples demonstrate how this model works, including an outline of learning outcomes, methods, and assessment for each session.

Example 1: Kickoff Meeting of MCoP

This kickoff session included an open invitation to all library staff members. Those who wished to attend registered via a short Google Form, which prompted e-mailing them a pre-session slide deck that included three main sections to review and a homework assignment that would drive the meeting's facilitated breakout sessions. Forty-five staff (out of just over 150 employees at the Hesburgh Libraries) registered for the session, and participants represented all programs at the library as well as the project management office. Attendance at this meeting showed that there was wide interest in metadata and an equally wide range of understanding and comfort with the domain area. There was general excitement at the chance to share insights and ask questions.

Some of the key takeaways from this session were the desire to have a shared vocabulary to level the playing field in discussions and to understand the source of records and the metadata ecosystem. Additionally, some interest was expressed in other key areas that support specific initiatives. These areas include serving patrons, ethical metadata practices, future metadata trends, metadata governance and stewardship, staff training, and metadata technologies. The meeting stimulated participants' interest in further learning, and MCoP members provided guidance on how to meet their needs with such programming.

Given that meetings were virtual, slide decks with the use of slide narration provided background information both verbally and visually to accommodate a large member base. An application called Padlet (padlet.com) provided an online bulletin board for posting prompts and responses from participants. The online bulletin board ensured a means of participation by those who were less comfortable expressing their thoughts or asking questions verbally. The homework exercise included some questions of reflection that were then used to start small-group discussions with a facilitator who had further question prompts and who took notes to capture members' feedback and level of understanding. The visioning exercise at the end of the session, via Padlet, provided a means to share participants' expectations for further learning.

The post-session assessment included the analysis of notes from the breakout sessions and the full-group discussion as a source for ideas on which to build a topic bank of issues for further programming or follow-up. The feedback surveys via Google Forms indicated that members felt at ease in the meeting, but there was a need to provide training on technical metadata jargon to facilitate ongoing conversations. The formats and use of Zoom, Padlet, and various online documents were successful in providing multiple ways for participation and follow-up by those in attendance, as well as those unable to make the session. The meeting outputs, including recordings and slides, became a permanent addition to the library staff portal. See figure 6.2 for a sample learning plan.

Learning Outcomes What participants will learn; our deliverables	Learning Methods Approaches for teaching and facilitating active learning during the meeting

• Understand the goals of the MCoP
 	
• Know how to get involved in the MCoP
 	
• Share how metadata impacts own work and work of others
 	
• Connect with MCoP members
	• Meeting invitation that articulate deliverables
	• Narrated, pre-session slide deck
	  ○ Key concepts of CoP
	  ○ The "what, why, and how" of the MCoP
	  ○ Ways to get involved in the MCoP
	  ○ Homework (two personal reflection questions for meeting breakout sessions)
	• Session slide deck
	  ○ Warm-up exercise via Padlet
	  ○ "When I say metadata, you say … "
	  ○ Meeting guidelines
	  ○ MCoP goals and guidelines for involvement
	  ○ "Getting your input" small-group discussions via Zoom breakout rooms
	  ○ Visioning exercise
	  ○ "If this were the best version of itself, where will MCoP be in one year?" via Padlet
	• Session script for presenters and technical assistants
	• Meeting recording posted to "document of documents" on staff portal

FIGURE 6.2
Example 1 learning plan

Example 2: Metadata Ecosystem: Part 1: Types of Metadata

Library staff received an open invitation for this session, along with a summary of members' feedback received to date, indicating the desire to understand the metadata ecosystem and its jargon. The context slide of the metadata ecosystem (figure 6.3) anchored this first of multiple sessions on the larger topic. Approximately thirty staff from throughout the libraries attended the virtual session held over Zoom.

During the session, the participants responded to an opening icebreaker and then learned about the broader context of the metadata ecosystem as outlined by the MCoP Governance Squad. Each layer of the ecosystem shown in figure 6.3 represents factors that influence understanding and decisions within our metadata domain.

- Review notes from break-out sessions.
- Review meeting logistics and success of technology used for the session.
- Review participant feedback from the Google Forms survey. Questions:
    - How relevant was the session content to your work?
    - Did the session improve your understanding of the topic?
    - Did you feel welcomed at the session, i.e., especially in the way concepts were introduced or by the language that was used?
    - How likely are you to join us again at a future meeting?
    - What went well about the session?
    - What would have made the session better?
    - What topics, questions, or concerns would you like covered in a future session?
    - Is there any additional feedback you would like to share?
- Create an Issue Bank to outline further ideas and initiatives, and gauge interest.
- Create a Document of Documents with key events and output resources for the community.

Metadata Ecosystem

Collections — Curated content that supports teaching and learning for the university community and the world at large

MCoP / Operations — Local practices applied to managing these collections through available systems with the help of metadata

Systems — Tools and places that support metadata creation, management, storage, preservation, discovery, and use

Metadata — Data about something that sometimes follows content (rules) or encoding standards and that can be categorized into different types, e.g., descriptive, access, technical, administrative, preservation, etc.

Source of Record / Source of Truth — Authoritative data source for a given data element / Trusted data source for an object as a whole

FIGURE 6.3
Metadata ecosystem

Most library staff can easily relate to the impact of our collections on the community, but underlying those collections are several technical layers. The figure highlighted the access and discovery of collections that depend on local practice, governance, and stewardship as managed by the MCoP and operations, as well as the systems used, the metadata created and managed, and the key level at the base, the source of record for our data. Two librarians from the Metadata Services program, Peggy Griesinger and Alex Papson, presented "Types of Metadata" (2021). After their presentation, which included many useful terms, definitions, and examples, Griesinger and Papson gave participants a pop quiz, which served as an in-class self-assessment of the concepts presented. The quiz reinforced the concepts and served to bolster the confidence of those new to the domain area. The participants also received a handout of terminology for use during the session. An open discussion and question period followed. Before leaving the meeting, action items were set,

FIGURE 6.4
Example 2 learning plan

Learning Outcomes What participants will learn; our deliverables	Learning Methods Approaches for teaching and facilitating active learning during the meeting	
• Have a common metadata vocabulary they can use • Understand the current state of our metadata ecosystem • Know that there are several types of metadata, each serving a different purpose • Know that there are many ways to form and work with our metadata	• Icebreaker via Padlet application • "When I was 10 years old, I thought I would grow up to be…" • Post meeting guidelines via single slide • Single-slide illustration of Metadata Ecosystem • Session slide deck • "Types of Metadata" (Griesinger and Papson 2021) • Typology of standards • Descriptive and access metadata • Other metadata types • Metadata structure and encoding • In-class quiz • Share slides with quiz questions • Use chat to record answers • Handout of "types of metadata" • Share via chat • Use handout during presentation and quiz	

which included asking members to provide more feedback on areas for further learning and asking participants to review the issues database and to add their name to topics of interest to them. See figure 6.4 for a sample learning plan.

This model of planning and conducting the meetings of the MCoP continued throughout the spring and summer of 2021. Community meetings included further work and discussion about the next steps the community should take to address the most pressing issues. As evident in the session examples and learning plans, the MCoP would start each meeting with some conceptual or foundational learning opportunities in order to create a common understanding, comfort, and trust among members. Members then pushed for deeper dives into issues and the development of specific projects to address identified areas of concern or topics for further training. Members also developed use cases of specific projects and shared them with the community for discussion and endorsement. These presentations served as mini-introductory learning

---

Learning Assessment
Review by MCoP Governance Squad of meeting and success of participant learning

- Review notes from break-out sessions.
- Review meeting logistics and success of technology used for the session.
- Review participant feedback from the Google Forms survey. Questions:
  - How relevant was the session content to your work?
  - Did the session improve your understanding of the topic?
  - Did you feel welcomed at the session, i.e., especially in the way concepts were introduced or by the language that was used?
  - How likely are you to join us again at a future meeting?
  - What went well about the session?
  - What would have made the session better?
  - What topics, questions, or concerns would you like covered in a future session?
  - Is there any additional feedback you would like to share?
- Review discussion and Q&A notes.
- Update Issue Bank to outline further ideas and initiatives, and gauge interest.
- Update Document of Documents with key events and output resources for the community.

sessions on topics such as mapping the source of record, persistent identifiers, and cataloging and discovery practice related to series. The projects that formed in this way received administrative approval prior to launching formal teams, and while stakeholder identification was a critical component of project formation, any member could join any of the project teams.

CONCLUSION

The problem to solve for the Hesburgh Libraries was how to cultivate a cross-organizational metadata strategy and practices to support the libraries' development and service goals. To meet this need, a community of practice provided an ideal model to allow broad reach in the metadata domain and to maintain respect for operational autonomy for specific collection work. With the framing provided by this model, learning was a natural outgrowth of forming the community of practice. Due to early stakeholder discussions that led to the formation of the MCoP structure, it was clear that discussion alone would not suffice to meet the standard of practice within the MCoP. The measures of success established in the MCoP's concept map made clear that governance, decision-making, and learning were all to be part of the community's work and culture. To make this happen, the MCoP Governance Squad's programming used a learning framework that includes identifying learning outcomes, methods, and assessment for each meeting, and listening carefully to member feedback as a means of determining the next steps to take. The future of the MCoP depends on two things: first, the motivation of members to continue to give time to learning in this area; and second, the continuing efforts of the MCoP Governance Squad to create learning opportunities using this successful framework to help members connect and learn within the metadata domain.

REFERENCES

Griesinger, Peggy, and Alexander Papson. 2021. "Types of Metadata." Hesburgh Libraries, Notre Dame University.

Hesburgh Libraries. n.d. "2013 State of the Libraries." Notre Dame University.

———. 2016. "This Week @ Hesburgh Libraries. 25 January." Notre Dame University.

———. 2018. "Defining a Transformative Research Library for the University of Notre Dame," 1–23. Notre Dame University.

———. 2020. "Hesburgh Libraries Reorganization." Notre Dame University.

Jain, Priti, and Stephen Mutula. 2008. "Libraries as Learning Organisations: Implications for Knowledge Management." *Library Hi Tech News* 25, no. 8: 10–14. doi: 10.1108/07419050810931273.

Marquardt, Michael J. 2020. "Building Learning Organizations with Action Learning." In *The Oxford Handbook of the Learning Organization*, edited by Anders Ortenblad. Oxford: Oxford University Press. doi: 10.1093/oxfordhb/9780198832355.001.0001.

Phipps, Shelley E. 1993. "Transforming Libraries into Learning Organizations." *Journal of Library Administration* 18, no. 3–4: 19–37. doi: 10.1300/J111v18n03_03.

Sarder, Russell. 2016. *Building an Innovative Learning Organization: A Framework to Build a Smarter Workforce, Adapt to Change, and Drive Growth*. Hoboken, NJ: John Wiley & Sons. doi: 10.1002/9781119235200.

Wenger, Etienne. 1998. *Communities of Practice: Learning, Meaning, and Identity.* New York: Cambridge University Press.

———. 2000. "Communities of Practice and Social Learning Systems." *Organization* 7, no. 2 (May): 225–46. doi: 10.1177/135050840072002.

7

Mind the (Training) Gap

A Case Study in Assessing Metadata Competences by Transforming Records for a Multi-System Migration

Dana Reijerkerk and Kristen J. Nyitray

OVER THE PAST THREE DECADES, THE EMERGENCE OF DIGITAL REPOSITORIES has required the skill sets of technical service professionals to adapt and evolve. Cataloging practice has enlarged from workflows focused on bibliographic description to metadata creation for the long-term preservation of digital assets. The skill sets required for this work are defined in various professional and technical publications; chief among these is "Core Competencies for Cataloging and Metadata Professional Librarians," or "Core Competencies for Cataloging" (Cataloging Competencies Task Force 2017), a document published by the Association for Library Collections & Technical Services as a supplement to the ALA's "Core Competences of Librarianship" (American Library Association 2009).

In libraries, metadata (data about data) is a collection development tool that embodies core library functions such as acquisitions, provenance, context, rights, and preservation. Metadata is comprised of three distinct interconnected types—descriptive, administrative, and structural—and ensures that the integrity of digital files is maintained (Library of Congress 2005). Metadata's prescribed architecture and construction of elements provides a mechanism for system-independent information retrieval and access. Integral to developing metadata records is adherence to best practices, controlled vocabularies, and standards, including Dublin Core semantic specifications (Dublin Core Metadata Initiative 2020). The implementation of these activities relies on an organization's investment and commitment to equipping staff with the knowledge and professional training needed to meet both technical benchmarks and stakeholder expectations.

This chapter discusses a multi-department collaborative project to reprocess digitized university art exhibition catalogs in an academic library at an R1 research university. It examines the challenges to legacy metadata remediation, the implications of a lack of training with migrations, and how to manage the expectations of internal repository stakeholders. Furthermore, it prioritizes the importance of organization-wide training in repository management, and positions a culture of continuous learning as a prerequisite for fulfilling the library's mission.

THE PILOT PROJECT'S CONTEXT

In 2020, the ongoing multi-system migration and system upgrade exposed a pressing need to reimagine training and institute workflows for repository management. Stony Brook University Libraries (SBUL) embarked on a pilot case study to assess the viability of migrating metadata from four legacy repositories to one platform, DSpace 6. This pilot project was undertaken to determine the challenges to migrating legacy digital assets, specifically the preparedness and readiness of staff to remediate metadata. The project was initiated by two librarians who possessed historical knowledge, technical expertise, and education in digital asset preservation. A digitized collection of university art exhibition catalogs was selected to test and study, on account of its finite extent of 127 items and its single-file format (PDFs).

To assess the readiness, preparedness, and competencies of cataloging and metadata professionals, the quality of legacy metadata was examined and the retrievability of digital items was tested. Through a phased assessment process, the findings were mapped to core skill sets for creating metadata records. The results identified and informed areas of training emphasis that needed investment at the organizational level. This study would also be used to make the case for the university to cover training costs and to increase its overall support for professional growth and development activities.

ASSESSMENT SOURCES AND FRAMEWORK

Several sources guided the pilot project's planning and framework. Two rapid-assessment benchmark reports for digital preservation were used to measure the state of SBUL's digital repositories (Reijerkerk 2020, 2021);

SBUL's digital assets librarian evaluated the digital preservation capabilities of the libraries in 2020-2021 using the Digital Preservation Coalition's maturity modeling tool, the Rapid Assessment Model (Digital Preservation Coalition, n.d.). Skill set competencies were drawn from the "Core Competencies for Cataloging" and the "Trustworthy Repositories Audit & Certification (TRAC) Criteria and Checklist," a best practice tool with metrics for assessing and auditing repositories (Center for Research Libraries and OCLC 2007). To improve the access and discoverability of its digital content, SBUL endeavored to transform the art exhibition catalogs' item-level records in adherence to accepted standards found in the "Dublin Core Metadata Best Practices" (Collaborative Digitization Program 2006). A six-part phased plan was developed for the assessment process:

Phase 1: Assessing the existing legacy metadata
Phase 2: Recording and diagnosing inconsistencies, errors, and
    absences in the metadata
Phase 3: Mapping the findings of phases 1 and 2 to core metadata skills
    and competencies
Phase 4: Identifying training gaps
Phase 5: Transforming the metadata
Phase 6: Articulating staff development needs and recommending
    training opportunities

Phase 1 centered on investigating the current state of item-level metadata in the records of the 127 art exhibition catalogs. This review included inspecting the types of metadata present and the elements, naming conventions, and data structures in each record. Phase 2 focused on pinpointing and logging errors and omissions in the records in consultation with DSpace documentation and accepted metadata standards. The item records were scrutinized for evidence of the three types of metadata as defined by the "Dictionary of Archives Terminology" (Society of American Archivists 2005-2021). Given the limited historical documentation available for the collection of art catalogs, several components of the digital asset life cycle were investigated: provenance, adherence to content standards, system functionality, and digital preservation actions. The findings of phases 1 and 2 were mapped in phase 3 to the skill and ability competencies delineated by the "Core Competencies for Cataloging" (Cataloging Competencies Task Force 2017). In phase 4, training and knowledge gaps were identified based on the standards articulated in the benchmark reports and from information compiled from the first three phases. (Figure 7.1 shows how knowledge gaps can be mapped to skills and core competencies.) Phase 5 concentrated on remediating the architecture for the record template, normalizing content, and adding enhanced-level cataloging elements. Finally, phase 6 outlined priorities and recommendations for staff training based on the totality of the assessment.

FIGURE 7.1
Mapping: Skills, competencies, and knowledge gaps

Skill & Ability Area	Core Competency	Knowledge Gaps	Examples
Application of conceptual frameworks, standards, and principles within a bibliographic system	Formulates consistent data by applying the Dublin Core metadata content standard	Inconsistent use of data element fields and content standards	Records with conflations of RDA, AACR2, and MARC standards
Application of conceptual frameworks, standards, and principles within a bibliographic system	Disambiguates creators, contributors, titles/series	Incorrect and/or inconsistent use of fields, naming conventions, subjects, and keywords	Artist names not represented in metadata; names of university and gallery applied inconsistently; authors omitted
Application of conceptual frameworks, standards, and principles within a bibliographic system	Analyzes and classifies resources	Uneven adherence to best practices for subject analysis and classification assignments	Records lacked LC subject headings and names; inconsistent use of metadata templates and element fields
Application of conceptual frameworks, standards, and principles within a bibliographic system	Encodes machine-actionable data	Inability to encode data	No serialization standards (XML, Turtle) used

Skill & Ability Area	Core Competency	Knowledge Gaps	Examples
Application of conceptual frameworks, standards, and principles within a bibliographic system	Asserts relationships between creators, works, etc.	Absence of publication information; lack of controlled vocabularies; lack of authorized names and subject headings	Entries for Toby Buonagurio appeared as "BUONAGURIO" and "Buonagurio"; lack of linkage; unsupported faceted searching
Application of universal standards within a local context	Assesses or seeks to understand local user needs for library metadata	Lack of accurate and consistent terminology for gallery names; minimal authority control for university-created publications	No consultation with art galleries staff or university archivist for local contexts
Application of universal standards within a local context	Sets (or advises on) local metadata practice, including selecting appropriate standards for local use	Working group disbanded; failed to develop digital project planning documents and local metadata practices	No consensus or guiding document for selecting and establishing local metadata practices
Application of universal standards within a local context	Documents local decisions and practices	Historical and current digital projects lack planning documentation	Projects lack coherence and consistency; unable to search across collections
Application of universal standards within a local context	Designs and modifies cataloging and metadata workflow processes	Policies and procedures yet to be developed	No formal workflows, processes, or guiding document for local metadata practices

(continued)

FIGURE 7.1 *(continued)*
Mapping: Skills, competencies, and knowledge gaps

Skill & Ability Area	Core Competency	Knowledge Gaps	Examples
Integration, mapping, and transformation of metadata within a bibliographic system	Converts or crosswalks a record/document from one meta-data standard to another	Inconsistent adherence to metadata stan-dards; inability to automate crosswalks of descriptive elements	Records include conflation of RDA, AACR2, MARC; lack of standardization hinders access
Integration, mapping, and transformation of metadata within a bibliographic system	Employs standards to normalize metadata	Metadata normalization done manually as prompted; no crosswalks developed	Dates not formatted as per the standard ISO 8601 expressed as YYYY-MM-DD; unsupported faceted searching
Integration, mapping, and transformation of metadata within a bibliographic system	Documents input and mapping decisions	Digitization proj-ects lack planning documentation; ad hoc decision-making	Provenance issues; inability to search across collections; metadata schemes are not interoperable

IDENTIFYING TRAINING GAPS AND OPPORTUNITIES

Information retrieval processes require well-formed metadata within a func-tional system that generates reliable results and supports faceted searching. Of the three types of metadata, descriptive metadata adds pathways for dis-covering library collections, while administrative and structural metadata establishes context, maintains provenance, and embeds preservation infor-mation. Together, these data document custodial history and aid life cycle management. Each of these activities is dependent on the staff's effectiveness and ability to create, develop, and maintain repositories and the assets they hold. In today's evolving technical services departments, a lack of technol-ogy skills does not need to be an obstacle; rather, this can be a development opportunity for designing a systematic training program based on continuing staff development in technical services (Davis 2016). One component of this could be the addition of training in team participation skills, such as goal-setting and measuring goal accomplishment (Zhu 2011). This would also aid in managing team expectations when embarking on the inevitable next migration or refreshing project. Targeted training in programming, systems, and digital asset management can substantially increase staff members' comfort with digital repository work. Professional development in the form of training, education, and mentoring is now expected when it comes to creating and preserving digital collections. According to the American Library Association (2012), "The transformation of libraries in the services offered and the perspective of their patrons, can only continue to progress if the staff of those libraries are encouraged to continue learning and working together." Moulaison-Sandy and Dykas (2016) suggest that librarians would be more likely to select and create documentation that adheres to the standards and best practices used by the institution, if relevant continuing education opportunities were more readily available to them.

At SBUL, ambiguities and conflations of staff roles and responsibilities, along with vacancies, originally prompted two librarians to initiate the pilot project. The project provided a forum for dialogues on planning, workflows, objectives, and outcomes. It also exposed gaps in organization-wide project management skills, since strategies and the resources needed to complete tasks were undocumented. More generally, creating a shared strategic plan for repositories can establish mutual understandings of long-term priorities and goals and will mitigate future migration problems, since "systems migrations are an inevitable necessity over time when needs and technology change" (Neatrour et al. 2017, 194). Such a plan also works to establish stakeholder expectations for future migrations.

In the pilot project, increasing the staff's awareness of accepted standards and best practice sources proved to be an essential element in remediating the metadata. Based on the evaluative findings of previous assessments, the data remediation and normalization needed to be done manually, since automated processing was unavailable. This work was performed by staff across departmental lines. More generally, metadata workflows can be improved with staff training focused on developing automated scripts for global edits, using controlled vocabularies, and adhering to DCMI Metadata Terms. Creating a custom tool similar to one developed by the University of Utah that performed metadata cleanup during the migration process (Neatrour et al. 2017) would support efficiency.

Learning and knowledge gaps were assessed against the "Core Competencies for Cataloging." In the future, a survey and manifest will record the self-perceived skill sets possessed by staff. The addition of a phase 7 will further identify gaps and help us to craft a plan of action in conjunction with the criteria of TRAC. We anticipate that future training areas will cover the application of universal standards at the local level and in the integration, mapping, and transformation of metadata within a bibliographic system. Until we establish a formal program, however, several free sources for continuing professional development are available to cataloging and metadata staff to improve and support the underlying needs of digital project initiatives and professional practice gaps: the Library of Congress's "Catalogers Learning Workshop" (Library of Congress 2021); the OLAC Catalogers Network's "Publications and Training" materials (OLAC Catalogers Network, n.d.); and the ALA's "Cataloging Tools and Resources" guide (American Library Association 2019). Moreover, the Digital Preservation Outreach and Education Network maintains an up-to-date list of trainings and provides consultations to develop individualized training plans (Digital Preservation Outreach and Education Network, n.d.).

CONCLUSION

Migration projects can afford libraries the opportunity to assess their benchmarks in digital asset management. Quality metadata is invaluable in a migration; it provides access to and control of digital files, bitstreams, and file formats. In libraries, technical services work has too often been dismissed as not intellectual or necessary to fulfill scholars' needs, in comparison to front-line public services (Laskowski and Maddox Abbott 2014). This narrative needs to be changed. Developing a culture of continuous learning with unequivocal support for professional development embedded within it can significantly further a library's aspirations to be a trusted digital repository. The life cycle management of digital files necessitates employing a staff with diverse skill sets. To build infrastructure and foster collegiality, organizational-wide training should incorporate the larger aims of digital initiatives and underscore the importance of individual contributions in meeting objectives. Defining roles, and the qualifications needed to implement and execute projects, institutes individual accountability and coherence among workflows. By framing training as an investment in staff and their career growth, gaps in knowledge can be closed. Consequently, a library's impact can be amplified, and its staff can be empowered to meaningfully contribute to its advancement.

REFERENCES

American Library Association. 2009. "ALA's Core Competences of Librarianship." www.ala.org/educationcareers/sites/ala.org.educationcareers/files/content/careers/corecomp/corecompetences/finalcorecompstat09.pdf.

———. 2012. "Staff Development." www.ala.org/tools/atoz/staff-development.

———. 2019. "Cataloging Tools and Resources: Home." https://libguides.ala.org/catalogingtools/.

Boylan, M. 2001. "Retrieval of Exhibition Catalogs: New Strategies at Virginia Commonwealth University." *Art Documentation: Journal of the Art Libraries Society of North America* 20, no. 2: 46–49.

Campbell, C. 1998. "Keeping It All Together: National Gallery of Canada Exhibition Records and Other Exhibition-Related Material." *Art Documentation: Journal of the Art Libraries Society of North America* 17, no. 2: 46–50.

Cataloging Competencies Task Force. 2017. "Core Competencies for Cataloging and Metadata Professional Librarians." Association for Library Collections & Technical Services. https://alair.ala.org/handle/11213/7853.

Center for Research Libraries and OCLC. 2007. "Trustworthy Repositories Audit & Certification (TRAC) Criteria and Checklist." Center for Research Libraries. www.crl.edu/sites/default/files/attachments/pages/trac_0.pdf.

Collaborative Digitization Program, CDP Metadata Working Group. 2006. "Dublin Core Metadata Best Practices Version 2.1.1." https://sustainableheritage network.org/digital-heritage/cdp-dublin-core-metadata-best-practices -version-21.

Davis, J. Y. 2016. "Transforming Technical Services: Evolving Functions in Large Research University Libraries." *Library Resources & Technical Services* 60, no. 1: 52–65. https://doi.org/10.5860/lrts.60n1.52.

Digital Preservation Coalition. n.d. "DPC Rapid Assessment Model." www.dpc online.org/digipres/dpc-ram.

Digital Preservation Outreach and Education Network. n.d. "Digital Preservation Outreach and Education Network." www.dpoe.network.

Dublin Core Metadata Initiative. 2020. "DCMI Metadata Terms." www.dublincore .org/specifications/dublin-core/dcmi-terms.

Laskowski, Mary S., and Jennifer A. Maddox Abbott. 2014. "The Evolution of Technical Services: Learning from the Past and Embracing the Future." *Technical Services Quarterly* 31, no. 1: 13–30. doi: 10.1080/07317131.2014.844619.

Library of Congress. 2005. "Library of Congress Digital Repository Development Core Metadata Elements." www.loc.gov/standards/metadata.html.

———. 2021. "Catalogers Learning Workshop." www.loc.gov/catworkshop/.

Mering, Margaret. 2019. "Transforming the Quality of Metadata in Institutional Repositories." *Serials Librarian* 76, no. 1–4: 79–82. doi: 10.1080/0361526X.2019.1540270.

Moulaison-Sandy, Heather, and Felicity Dykas. 2016. "High-Quality Metadata and Repository Staffing: Perceptions of United States-Based OpenDOAR Participants." *Cataloging & Classification Quarterly* 54, no. 2: 101–16. doi: 10.1080/ 01639374.2015.1116480.

Neatrour, Anna, Jeremy Myntti, Matt Brunsvik, Harish Maringanti, Brian McBride, and Alan Witkowski. 2017. "A Clean Sweep: The Tools and Processes of a Successful Metadata Migration." *Journal of Web Librarianship* 11, no. 3–4: 194–208. doi: 10.1080/19322909.2017.1360167.

OLAC Catalogers Network. n.d. "Publications and Training Materials." www.olac inc.org/training-publications.

Reijerkerk, Dana. 2020. "Digital Asset Inventory: Report on Digital Preservation Issues at Stony Brook University Libraries." Stony Brook University Libraries, State University of New York at Stony Brook.

———. 2021. "Digital Asset Assessment: Second Annual Report on Digital Preservation Issues at Stony Brook University Libraries." Stony Brook University Libraries, State University of New York at Stony Brook.

Rinaldo, K. 2007. "Evaluating the Future: Special Collections in Art Libraries." *Art Documentation: Journal of the Art Libraries Society of North America* 26, no. 2: 38–47.

Salomon, K. 2014. "Facilitating Art-Historical Research in the Digital Age: The Getty Research Portal." *Getty Research Journal* 6: 137–41. doi: 10.1086/675796.

Society of American Archivists. 2005–2021. "Dictionary of Archives Terminology." https://dictionary.archivists.org.

Zhu, Lihong. 2011. "Use of Teams in Technical Services in Academic Libraries." *Library Collections, Acquisitions, & Technical Services* 35, no. 2–3. doi: 10.1016/ j.lcats.2011.03.013.

8

Looking Back to Move Forward

Future-Proofing Staff through Skill Development

Tammie Busch and Marlee Graser

BY 2019, THE CATALOGING UNIT OF THE LOVEJOY LIBRARY AT SOUTHERN Illinois University Edwardsville (SIUE) had faced most of the challenges that technical services departments often experience. In the preceding three years the Lovejoy Library Technical Services department, of which the Cataloging unit is a substantial part, had experienced considerable staff and faculty turnover, including the retirement of the library's long-term technical services director. A recent faculty addition to the Technical Services department, Marlee Graser, served as the cataloging unit's interim supervisor for eight months until the hiring of a new catalog and metadata librarian. Part of her interim role was to perform a needs assessment to help streamline the transition to a new supervisor when a permanent replacement could be hired. Tammie Busch joined the Technical Services department as the new, permanent supervisor of the Cataloging unit in July 2019 and, in collaboration with Marlee, began a systematic review of the Cataloging unit, its work, and its staff. The staff's position descriptions indicated that they were responsible for high-level, autonomous work that relied on a deep understanding of current cataloging standards. But after meeting with the catalogers and reviewing their day-to-day work, this was actually not found to be the case. For over fifteen years, original cataloging and the development of local best practices had been done exclusively by the faculty librarians in the unit. The staff were mainly working as copy catalogers. Additionally, these staff catalogers had been working in an environment that had not empowered or rewarded problem-solving, taking on new challenges, or engaging in self-directed learning; this resulted in a substantial skills gap and an unbalanced division of labor.

As the dust settled after the high turnover of the previous three years, the remaining cataloging staff were now increasingly being asked to problem-solve autonomously and perform high-level cataloging. And it was no surprise that, in discussions with each staff member, they said that they were burnt out, bored, and undertrained. They wanted new, more challenging responsibilities but were struggling with how to self-direct their own work and learning. Tammie recognized that the permanent reduction in cataloging personnel, in addition to major upcoming projects, like a consortium-wide library service platform (LSP) migration, would demand a great deal of learning and adapting from everyone. Developing the cataloging staff's skills in self-directed learning and thus empowering them to continuously improve and take on new challenges would be essential to the success of their work. Over the next two years, Tammie used core concepts of adult learning theory from Malcolm Knowles and Lev Vygotsky to develop and support the staff's self-directed learning skills.

SELF-DIRECTED LEARNING

The concept of self-directed learning was originally defined by Knowles in the 1970s and built upon the methods and principles used in adult education. Knowles defines self-directed learning as a process "in which individuals take the initiative, with or without the help of others, in diagnosing their learning needs, formulating learning goals, identifying human and material resources for learning, choosing and implementing appropriate learning strategies, and evaluating those learning outcomes" (1975, 18). Additionally, Knowles includes a critical first step of "climate setting, that is, creating an atmosphere of mutual respect and support" to guide staff toward becoming self-directed learners (Merriam and Bierema 2014, 63). Where Knowles provided the steps, Vygotsky's theories on social constructivism and scaffolded instruction provided the framework for our unit's actual retraining and education. Vygotsky's theory of the "zone of proximal development" (ZPD) is defined as "the distance between the actual development level as determined by independent problem solving and the level of potential development as determined through problem solving under guidance or in collaboration with more capable peers"

(1978, 86). In essence, Vygotsky theorized that learning occurs when lessons are scaffolded on learning that has already been achieved in an environment with the support of peers.

Vygotsky's theories emphasize the importance of the relationship between the teacher and the student, and the social context and intersubjectivity of learning (Smagorinsky 2018). These are particularly important in the first step of Knowles's process for becoming a self-directed learner. Tammie knew that mutual respect and support would be imperative. The cataloging staff already recognized their knowledge gaps, which made setting the climate much easier. The staff had also worked together for a minimum of fifteen years and were very invested in each other's success. Vygotsky (1962) believed that social interaction is an integral part of learning, and situated learning, a theory that follows from Vygotskian theory, creates meaning from real, daily activities (Stein 1998, para. 2). The staff's collaborative approach to learning, in which they offered each other support, modeled the expansion of Vygotsky's theory of the "zone of proximal development" by Moll and Whitmore (1993). This expansion proposes a "collective zone of proximal development" that emphasizes the collaborative effort between teachers and students in learning success. By recognizing the importance of the social context in learning, Tammie was able to create an environment of mutual respect and support within the group that increased engagement and built trust.

DEVELOPING A TRAINING PLAN

Diagnosing the staff's learning needs was a little more challenging. One of the major issues that Tammie faced was a sustained culture that discouraged autonomous problem-solving and disincentivized taking initiative. The major, high-level goal was to develop the staff as self-directed learners by getting them interested in their work, feeling comfortable when problem-solving on their own, and being prepared for organizational change. Tammie also recognized that there were pressing practical problems that also needed to be addressed. First, each cataloger was assigned predictive and prescriptive cataloging work based on a specific format of materials. But as the department shrank and moved away from format-specific cataloging assignments, staff catalogers needed a broader understanding of cataloging that could be applied to materials of any format when the need arose. Rather than give them the same prescriptive training they had experienced in the past, an important learning goal was to teach them why they catalog, not simply how to catalog. As a member of a statewide library consortium, SIUE's library is required to meet specific cataloging standards and practices. Therefore, foundational cataloging knowledge and aligning our practices to the consortium's standards would be essential. Additionally, the consortium had purchased and prioritized a migration of its statewide library system from Ex Libris Voyager, which had been in place for over fifteen years, to Ex Libris Alma. Alma is a next-generation LSP in which most records are part of a larger network of shared bibliographic records. Not only did the staff need to learn an entirely new library system, but for the first time, their cataloging work would be open to review and reuse by ninety-one other libraries in the consortium.

Part and parcel of the work of choosing and implementing appropriate learning strategies is identifying the extant human and material resources for learning. Our training material resources were abundant. Between free trainings accessible through OCLC, the Library of Congress, Ex Libris, and the consortium, Tammie had plenty of materials to work with. However, the human resources were less plentiful. Marlee was busy coordinating the library's system migration single-handedly, so Tammie needed to formulate a plan to train and educate the staff in the practical and technical competencies for the work that lay ahead while also guiding and developing the staff's skills in self-directed learning. These competencies would address the needs of both our consortial and local practices. The practical competencies focused on answering the question "How or when do I . . . ?" and included learning how to use Connexion macros to make cataloging work more efficient, and learning how and when to enhance bibliographic records using format-specific local best practices. The technical competencies focused on answering the question "Why do I . . . ?" These competencies included understanding how incorporating RDA elements in our bibliographic records supports discovery, understanding the advantages of OCLC's cooperative cataloging environment, and the importance of sharing our work with the wider cataloging community.

Tammie had already determined that collaborative and situated learning, in which the staff could pool their knowledge, ask each other questions, and create meaning from real daily activities, would be essential to the learning strategies that she would use. She also knew that she would be using scaffolded instruction based on Vygotsky's ZPD theory, in which each lesson and learning outcome would build on what the staff already knew or had just learned. Specifically, the cataloging lessons would take a back-to-basics approach to reaffirm the foundations of cataloging praxis while also focusing on how the catalogers' work impacts library user experience and aligns with the library's vision and mission. Starting simply, the lessons would also use work or workflows that the staff were already familiar with to teach them that they could apply that knowledge in new and different technologies and contexts. After working with the staff for several months, Tammie was also aware that they learned best by seeing, doing, and reviewing. Each lesson integrated different methods of the same structure: a group or video tutorial (seeing) that incorporated hands-on learning to demonstrate how the lesson would or could be applied in their daily work (doing), and documentation to review and continue to reference after the lessons. The lessons also included existing lesson plans that are freely available online, such as OCLC Connexion training (https://help.oclc.org/Metadata_Services/Connexion/Connexion_client_training), which Tammie supplemented with face-to-face instruction. She also created original lesson plans, such as the one she created for Alma training (see figure 8.1) that was implemented during the pandemic's stay-at-home order, and she supplemented these with Zoom instruction sessions.

One of the first learning opportunities occurred with the implementation of a cataloging workflow Trello board (see figure 8.2). Trello is a collaborative project management tool that organizes projects into boards, lists, and cards. The staff were asked to add each item they were cataloging to a card on the Trello board and use the lists to indicate the status of their work. None of the cataloging staff had used Trello before or been asked to make their work so public. After a group tutorial on Trello that included hands-on learning to use it in their daily workflow, Tammie gave the staff some basic documentation, encouraged them to ask questions as needed, and sent them on their way. Trello was a great lesson in how to apply knowledge or information that they already knew (their work assignments) into a new system or tool. It also eased them into making their work and the bibliographic records more public and open to peer evaluation, starting small so that they would be more prepared and comfortable for the transition to Alma's shared network of bibliographic records. Trello also enabled the staff to start their learning journey with success and achieve a high-level learning outcome, thus reaffirming that they were capable of learning new things.

Training in Alma (Part 1): Review Training Videos

Note: All videos can be found at https://knowledge.exlibrisgroup.com/Alma/
Training/Alma_Essentials.

Orientation
- Introduction to Alma training (11 min)
- Introduction to Alma (12 min)

Navigation and Searching
- Navigating in Alma (10 min)
  » Hands-on: Refamiliarize yourself with the Alma homepage.
    - Review menu options across top of page.
    - Review search options.
  » Look at options under "physical titles" and "physical items."
    - Review task list (clipboard icon in blue bar at top of page).
    - Find help menu (question mark in circle icon).
- Searching in Alma (7 min)
  (Searching in Alma online help page)
  » Hands-on: Spend some time doing some searches in Alma in both the IZ and the NZ.
  » Hands-on: Explore the search results page.
    - Start with an All titles, Title search of Harry Potter in the IZ.
      – Limit your search results by physical books from the facets on the left side of the page.
      – Are there any titles we do not own? How do you know?
      – Review the inventory information for a title from the search results page.
      – Look at the Record View of one of your search results. Go back to your search results.
      – Look at the List of Holdings page for one of your search results. Go back to your search results.
      – Look at the List of Items page for one of your search results.
        » From this page, go to the Physical Item Editor.
      – Display one of your search results in Discovery.
      – EXPLORE!

FIGURE 8.1
Alma training lesson plan—Using technology for learning

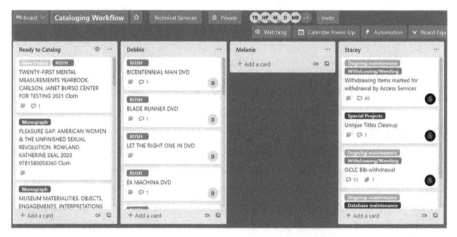

FIGURE 8.2
Cataloging workflow Trello board

Learning Trello eased the staff's concerns over learning something new, so Tammie moved on to the next learning goal of back-to-basics cataloging, to expand their cataloging knowledge and ensure that they were following consortium standards for cataloging practice. The consortium's guidelines encourage catalogers to enhance access and description in bibliographic records when appropriate and to make sure enhancements are reflected in WorldCat, not just locally. An additional requirement is that all original cataloging must be done through OCLC. Perhaps because of their unfamiliarity with OCLC's Connexion or their limited cataloging knowledge, the staff were not following these guidelines regularly. Tammie implemented mandatory training using OCLC's nine-module Connexion client training, and supplemented the training with face-to-face review sessions and documentation available from OCLC. Their training progress was tracked using Trello (see figure 8.3). During review sessions, the staff worked through examples collaboratively to demonstrate that they were able to apply what they had learned, and they asked questions when there was any confusion. The face-to-face review sessions also allowed Tammie to discuss the relevance of specific cataloging work and how it aligns with discovery, access, and user experience; she thus balanced the narrative within the lessons between how to do something and why we do a particular thing. The lessons in cataloging using Connexion training reintroduced staff to the problem-solving resources they were already familiar with but had not been encouraged to use. Problems that had previously been forwarded to faculty librarians could now often be solved autonomously by reviewing a core set of resources.

Because Alma was such an extreme transition from the old ILS, Tammie and Marlee originally thought that it would present the most challenging learning curve. But by the time the staff had reached the point to begin learning Alma, Tammie knew that the training methods used for the previous lessons worked well for them. However, early in 2020, the COVID-19 pandemic forced all university personnel to begin working remotely. Face-to-face Alma trainings had to be replaced by self-paced, asynchronous lessons supplemented with Zoom review sessions. Tammie provided the staff with hands-on activities and clearly defined procedures to follow. However, there is more than one way to do just about anything in Alma, and a frequent staff comment in review sessions was, "You can also do it this way." This comment gave Tammie an "Aha!"

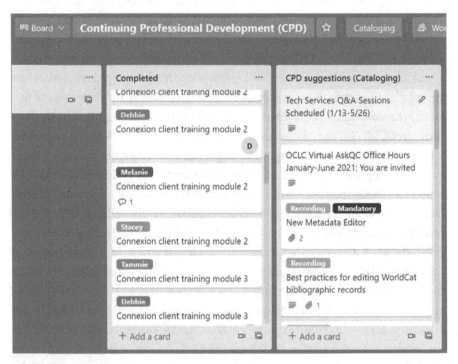

FIGURE 8.3
Continuing professional development Trello board

moment. The staff had reached a point where the lines between practical and high-level goals had been blurred, demonstrating the ever-evolving nature of Vygotsky's ZPD. As the staff's actual development had grown, the zone of proximal development had also expanded, leading to a continued potential for learning (Vygotsky 1978). Everything that the staff had learned up to this point had prepared them for this moment. As a result, the Alma lessons, and all future learning, transitioned from prescriptive to self-directed, from "this is how you do it" to "this is what you need to know to learn or accomplish the task at hand." Achieving this learning threshold was best exemplified by how prepared the staff were when there was a rapid revision to the Alma cataloging tool, which changed where tasks were located, but not the higher-level process. Prior to hitting the learning threshold, Tammie had written out step-by-step directions that the staff could review and use as a reference outside of the lessons. But after hitting the learning threshold, Tammie rewrote the documentation to describe the goals of and guidelines for accomplishing specific tasks, knowing that the staff would be able to fill in the gaps and troubleshoot the process on their own. This approach has also prepared them for inevitable changes or updates to the system in the future.

Although Alma was the most pressing learning goal, it turned out to be less of a challenge than originally thought. By leveraging Vygotsky's "method of teaching that credits the student with the power to become an active learner," each lesson also built the capacity of the staff to identify areas for their own development, create goals, seek out resources, and implement learning strategies on their own (von Glasersfeld and Smith 1996, 25). The result of the process was to build a collective mindset of active and self-directed learning and to give ownership of learning, and ultimately of the unit and its work, back to the staff. Tammie and Marlee continue to see the success of this work in the staff's enthusiasm for learning and their participation in its process. For example, when remote work left Tammie feeling as though she was losing organic teaching moments, she implemented a weekly fifteen-minute "Wednesday Lesson" via Zoom. Initially, Tammie chose and delivered the lessons herself, but over time, the staff have become much more vocal about what they want to learn, and have even started teaching Wednesday Lessons themselves to share skills they have developed or new tools they have discovered.

SUCCESSFUL OUTCOMES

The last step in Knowles's guide to self-directed learning is evaluating learn-ing outcomes. While evaluation has been a continuous part of our training process, the clearest evidence that the process has been a success came in the first months of 2021. In January 2021, the Lovejoy Library Technical Services department was reorganized into the Systems and Discovery department and Marlee was hired on a one-year contract as the department's coordinator. A big part of her work was to assess the work and workflows of everyone in the department and coordinate changes designed to streamline our processes. While assessing the department, it became clear that the division of labor was considerably unbalanced across the operational areas within the department. Cataloging, while still relatively unsupported, had been consistently staffed. Digital collection metadata and database maintenance were chronically depri-oritized and had virtually no personnel dedicated to it. Because the department had not been approved to hire new staff to cover operational gaps, Tammie and Marlee had to think creatively about using existing skill sets and retrain-ing the staff that they already had. Initially, they entered this process with a bit of trepidation. The staff in the Cataloging unit had been through so many changes over the past two years that Tammie and Marlee were worried that they would be fatigued by the process. In practice, the exact opposite proved to be true. The scaffolded professional development led by Tammie reaffirmed that, with the appropriate amount of support from departmental leadership, the staff were capable of taking on anything. Their confidence in their own skills had grown exponentially, and more importantly, their confidence in their ability to take on new responsibilities and face challenges with a growth mindset made implementing departmental changes much more successful.

REFERENCES

Knowles, Malcolm. 1975. *Self-Directed Learning: A Guide for Learners and Teachers.* New York: Association Press.

Merriam, Sharan B., and Laura L. Bierema. 2014. *Adult Learning: Linking Theory and Practice.* San Francisco: John Wiley & Sons.

Moll, Luis C., and Kathryn F. Whitmore. 1993. "Vygotsky in Classroom Practice: Moving from Individual Transmission to Social Transaction." In *Contexts for Learning: Sociocultural Dynamics in Children's Development*, edited by Ellice

A. Forman, Norris Minick, and C. Addison Stone, 19–42. New York: Oxford University Press.

Smagorinsky, Peter. 2018. "Deconflating the ZPD and Instructional Scaffolding: Retranslating and Reconceiving the Zone of Proximal Development as the Zone of Next Development." *Learning, Culture and Social Interaction* 16: 70–75. http://dx.doi.org/10.1016/j.lcsi.2017.10.009.

Stein, David. 1998. "Situated Learning in Adult Education." ERIC Clearinghouse on Adult, Career, and Vocational Education (ED418250). www.edpsycinteractive .org/files/sitadlted.html.

von Glasersfeld, Ernst, and Leslie Smith. 1996. "Chapter 2: Learning and Adaptation in the Theory of Constructivism." In *Critical Readings on Piaget*, edited by Leslie Smith, 20–27. London: Routledge.

Vygotsky, Lev S. 1962. *Thought and Language*. Cambridge, MA: MIT Press.

———. 1978. *Mind in Society: The Development of Higher Psychological Processes*. Cambridge, MA: Harvard University Press.

Circulation Services Training in a Remote Work Environment

A Case Study of UTM Library's Library Services Platform Migration during a Pandemic

Mai Lu

WHEN THE UNIVERSITY OF TORONTO LIBRARIES (UTL) BEGAN PLANNING to migrate to a new library services platform (LSP), they did not anticipate training and launching the new system in the middle of a global pandemic. The LSP affects every department within each of the libraries across the UTL system. Various workflows carry materials through acquisitions, invoicing, cataloging, discovery, and circulation.

UTL is composed of over forty libraries, spread across three campuses. The University of Toronto Mississauga Library (UTML) is one of the campus libraries within UTL. The University of Toronto Mississauga (UTM) serves over 15,200 undergraduate students and 900 graduate students across more than 180 programs and 90 areas of study (University of Toronto Mississauga, n.d.).

In November 2019, the UTL's LSP project lead and communications coordinator visited UTML and presented the plan to launch the new LSP in August 2020. The original plan was to provide staff training in the spring-summer and go live with the new system in August 2020. However, the COVID-19 pandemic changed these plans. In March 2020, under the guidance of public health and the university, all the UTL locations closed due to the pandemic. In late June, most libraries reopened for limited services, as permitted by local public health authorities and the university administration. The LSP launch date was postponed to January 2021, and training plans were modified to be delivered for a remote work environment. The LSP training team and functional groups developed asynchronous training modules, including online videos and practice exercises, as well as synchronous sessions for questions and demonstrations.

This chapter will provide a case study on how UTML's Information and Loans Service (ILS), the library's circulation services team, learned how to utilize the new LSP, through remote learning, during the pandemic. The chapter will examine the challenges and opportunities that arose from remote training. In addition to training provided by the LSP team, the ILS team at UTML introduced local practices to ensure that staff understood the training materials.

CHALLENGES

The training presented several challenges. In addition to the challenges inherent in training staff in a new circulation module for a new LSP, the pandemic contributed additional layers of complexity to the training.

Circulation services is a team-oriented, hands-on service involving significant materials handling. Checking materials out to patrons, checking items in upon return, processing overdue fees, and registering new patrons are in-person, hands-on activities. Traditionally, circulation services' training is conducted in person, either one-on-one or in small groups, with a handful of training accounts and a cart of books. However, the public health authorities mandated physical distancing of two meters (approximately six feet) between individuals. This was a significant barrier to providing in-person instruction on the circulation modules.

Learning a new LSP can be challenging for staff. UTL had been using Sirsi Workflows for eighteen years. Many staff had worked exclusively with this system during their library career. Atkins (2004, 78) has described how staff members' level of comfort in learning new systems may vary, and how it is important to factor in the psychological impact on the staff of learning a new system. Atkins (86) also noted that staff's level of comfort with computers may vary. Some staff are very web savvy and can move through modules quickly, while others less confident in their computer skills may require more personal coaching. Working remotely can amplify these concerns, since staff would need to learn the skills on their own.

The UTL system is large, and with over forty libraries, there are variations in local practices. The training provided for the system would probably need to be adapted to suit the needs of individual libraries. Atkins (2004, 79) stated that while variations can exist between libraries, system-wide training can provide the core competencies required to utilize a new system.

OPPORTUNITIES

While there were many challenges, UTL and UTML identified several opportunities to improve on their traditional circulation training. They presented a multipronged solution to training remotely that included self-directed learning, online learning modules, and team-oriented training opportunities. Communication was critical throughout the process. The LSP coordinator e-mailed weekly updates with information about training, configuration changes, and timelines in order to keep everyone informed and engaged.

Learning from other libraries that had recently migrated to Ex Libris Alma had already begun before the pandemic, and was adapted when the travel restrictions began. UTL sought out expertise from libraries that had recently migrated to Alma. UTL staff attended the State University of New York Library Association's virtual conference in February 2020. UTL itself hosted an LSP Summit in March 2020 with guest speakers from Harvard University, the University of Minnesota, the University of Southern California, and Western Libraries in Ontario. The LSP Summit had originally been planned as an in-person event. As concerns about the pandemic grew and institutions restricted travel for their staff, the event became a hybrid of in-person (for staff on the main campus) and virtual (for staff from other campuses) gatherings in order to limit the number of people in the training room.

SELF-DIRECTED LEARNING

Self-directed learning was a key part of the training program. This was composed of Ex Libris videos and asynchronous training modules created by the LSP functional teams. UTL made use of the "Getting to Know Alma" online training modules through the Ex Libris Knowledge Center. Completing the modules and passing the quiz awarded staff access to the LSP sandbox. The sandbox allowed staff to practice performing circulation functions in a test environment. Practice and experimentation were thereby encouraged. The first sandbox contained Ex Libris test data, while subsequent sandboxes contained UTL data and configurations, which allowed for a more familiar practice environment.

Various online training modules were developed, including videos, handouts in PDF, and practice exercises. The LSP functional groups created short videos introducing the new system and demonstrating how to perform specific functions on it. When communicating a large amount of information, it is advisable to break up the information into smaller doses to allow employees to absorb the information more effectively (Michalak and Rysavy 2018, 295). There were two introductory modules developed for everyone, followed by a stream of training modules for specific functional areas, as shown in figure 9.1.

FIGURE 9.1
LSP asynchronous training modules on Quercus (course management system)

Circulation services is part of the Fulfillment functional area within Alma. There were training modules developed on patron records, loans, fines and fees, requests, and curbside pickup routines (see figure 9.2). Video tutorials have been used successfully in library training for many years. McKenna (2020) noted that using videos for training significantly reduced the amount of hands-on training time required. This enabled the trainers to focus on answering questions about the training material rather than on presenting the information. Each LSP video included a training script that functioned as a handout with the steps written out (see figure 9.3). Staff could refer to either the video or handout when practicing the steps themselves. There were also practice exercises (see figure 9.4) that provided hands-on experience. Staff watched the videos at their own pace while working from home. They could pause the video while practicing the workflow in the sandbox, and they could rewatch the videos as many times as needed.

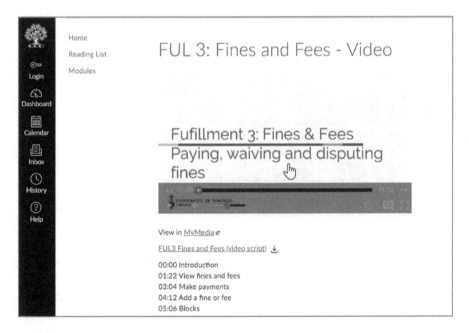

FIGURE 9.2
Fulfillment training video on fines and fees, with video script and timestamps

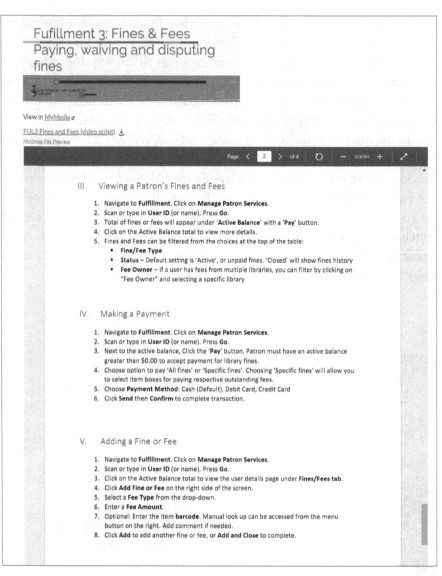

Fulfillment 3: Fines & Fees
Paying, waiving and disputing
fines

View in MyMedia

FUL3 Fines and Fees (video script)

Minimize File Preview

Page < 2 > of 4 ↻ — ZOOM + ↗

III.   Viewing a Patron's Fines and Fees

1. Navigate to **Fulfillment**. Click on **Manage Patron Services**.
2. Scan or type in **User ID** (or name). Press **Go**.
3. Total of fines or fees will appear under **'Active Balance'** with a **'Pay'** button.
4. Click on the Active Balance total to view more details.
5. Fines and Fees can be filtered from the choices at the top of the table:
   * **Fine/Fee Type**
   * **Status** – Default setting is 'Active', or unpaid fines. 'Closed' will show fines history
   * **Fee Owner** – If a user has fees from multiple libraries, you can filter by clicking on "Fee Owner" and selecting a specific library

IV.   Making a Payment

1. Navigate to **Fulfillment**. Click on **Manage Patron Services**.
2. Scan or type in **User ID** (or name). Press **Go**.
3. Next to the active balance, Click the **'Pay'** button. Patron must have an active balance greater than $0.00 to accept payment for library fines.
4. Choose option to pay 'All fines' or 'Specific fines'. Choosing 'Specific fines' will allow you to select item boxes for paying respective outstanding fees.
5. Choose **Payment Method**: Cash (Default), Debit Card, Credit Card
6. Click **Send** then **Confirm** to complete transaction.

V.   Adding a Fine or Fee

1. Navigate to **Fulfillment**. Click on **Manage Patron Services**.
2. Scan or type in **User ID** (or name). Press **Go**.
3. Click on the Active Balance total to view the user details page under **Fines/Fees tab**.
4. Click **Add Fine or Fee** on the right side of the screen.
5. Select a **Fee Type** from the drop-down.
6. Enter a **Fee Amount**.
7. Optional: Enter the Item **barcode**. Manual look up can be accessed from the menu button on the right. Add comment if needed.
8. Click **Add** to add another fine or fee, or **Add and Close** to complete.

FIGURE 9.3
Fulfillment training scripts that accompanied training videos and could be used as a handout on loans and returns

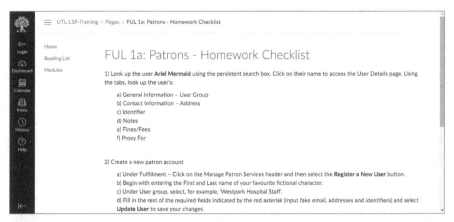

FIGURE 9.4
Fulfillment training homework exercise on searching and creating patron records

VIRTUAL SYNCHRONOUS LEARNING

Epps et al. described using in-person workshops to supplement learning from online videos so that staff members could acquire "face-to-face experience with the interpersonal aspects of the course and gain insight into topics that were not well covered in the online component" (2016, 203). In addition to self-directed training, the LSP team provided group sessions by functional area using videoconferencing software (Zoom and Microsoft Teams). Following the release of the asynchronous videos, there were live, or synchronous, sessions held where staff could ask questions and members of the functional team demonstrated various workflows. These sessions were held via Zoom. Following the launch of Alma in January 2021, the LSP team set up a series of "Ask Me Anything" (AMA) sessions and grouped the sessions for user services and technical services personnel. These sessions were held using Microsoft Teams. Zoom was used for the first set of group sessions, since it allowed for a greater number of participants. Teams was used for the second set of group sessions because it allowed participants to refer back to links shared in the Teams chat following the session.

Following on the success of the AMAs, when launching the curbside pickup service using Alma, the LSP team created a Teams channel for staff to ask questions and receive real-time assistance. The staff appreciated this real-time connection to the experts.

LOCAL TRAINING SUPPORT

As the University of Toronto Libraries is a large organization with many libraries, each with its own local circulation practices, the LSP training provided by the UTL covered the functionality of the Alma system. Local teams determined how Alma would function for their library workflows. The UTML team implemented training strategies to ensure that staff members understood and could successfully apply the information learned in the training. Communication, encouragement, and recognition were the cornerstones of this training strategy. Atkins stated that "in addition to providing skills training and instruction in essential information about the system, a successful training program will also attend to the psychological impact the new system may have on the staff" (2004, 78). Change can be hard for staff; and change during a pandemic can be even more challenging.

Communication was identified early on as a key to success. Leading up to the Alma training, the team meetings doubled in frequency, from weekly to twice per week. This made it possible for one weekly meeting to discuss library operations, and one weekly meeting to discuss the Alma training. This ensured that the Alma training did not get lost in periods when there was a lot of operational information to share or discuss. It was critical that communication flowed between team members and not just from the supervisors to the team. Team members were encouraged to voice their concerns, ask questions, and raise issues they encountered in the new system.

Before the pandemic, the LSP team watched the "Getting to Know Alma" videos together in the conference room. Team members were encouraged to watch the videos independently as well. As a group, they could pause a video as needed and discuss different functions of the system. Staff were encouraged to ask questions in this small-group environment. During the pandemic, the team discussed the training materials in virtual staff meetings using Zoom's screen share functionality. Everyone was encouraged to ask questions and share any concerns as they went along.

As a front-line service, it is critical for circulation services to be delivered seamlessly (Atkins 2004, 79). Our circulation services staff take pride in being able to operate the LSP expertly to provide excellent customer service. To gain this level of comfort with a new system, the staff needed to practice, practice, practice.

ON-THE-JOB PRACTICE

When it was safe to do so, in compliance with the public health authorities and the university, some staff were allowed to return to work in the UTM Library. This provided an opportunity for them to practice using Alma in the library. Staff wore face masks and practiced physical distancing when in the library. At UTML the team worked in weekly rotations, with a new pair of staff working each week. This allowed everyone to have a turn working hands-on with checking materials in, checking them out, and navigating issues. Staff were encouraged to ask questions as they used the modules in person, and to share their learning with the rest of the team during the virtual staff meetings.

Active participation was not only encouraged, but it was also recognized and celebrated. The team gave credit to staff members when they identified issues of concern or raised questions that had not come up before. The team was reminded that they were all in this together—all learning the new system together.

Because circulation services is a team-oriented service, it was important to UTML to celebrate milestones together, even when most staff were working remotely and only a few staff members were in the library at a time. Staff took photos of the first day of curbside pickup, the first book checked in using Alma, the first inter-campus delivery requested through Alma, and more. These photos were shared with the team in the staff newsletter.

By increasing opportunities for communication, encouraging team members to participate actively, and recognizing individual and team contributions, the team addressed the psychological impact of staff learning a new system, while also supporting skills training and learning and retaining information about the new system. These strategies improved staff members' learning, eased anxiety, and helped them feel more comfortable with the new system.

BENEFITS OF BLENDED LEARNING

While the pandemic threw a wrench into the implementation and training plans for the new LSP, there were unforeseen benefits to learning in a remote work environment. The staff could learn at their own pace using the online training modules. The online modules created a safe space for staff to practice, make mistakes, and learn the new circulation module.

One of the most significant advantages of using a flipped classroom approach is that people can learn at their own pace. The staff could view the training videos and pause, rewind, replay sections, or use subtitles as needed. Traditional circulation training would typically involve an instructor demonstrating how to perform specific functions in the system. In classroom environments, when participants are given time to practice, it is often time limited, which can be stressful for participants who don't grasp the material quickly. In contrast, using the online training modules, staff could complete the practice exercises on their own, at their own pace. In traditional classroom training, if participants have questions after the session, they would follow up with the instructor, and the instructor would need to demonstrate that function again. With the online training modules, the staff could review the asynchronous material as often as needed. The Q&A sessions following the training and the AMA sessions after launch allowed staff members to ask specific questions as they worked with the new system.

The flipped classroom also created a safe space for staff who would consider themselves slow learners or less technologically savvy. The combination of videos and written documentation supported different learning styles. People who learn better by working independently could take the time they needed to reflect and practice. People who learn better in groups could participate in team meetings and ask questions in the AMA sessions. Epps et al. (2016, 207) stated the importance of providing training materials in a variety of learning methods to allow for different learning styles and needs.

Retention of information has been documented as a concern when using the traditional training method. Michalak and Rysavy (2018, 292) noted that staff who received face-to-face training and were provided with a print procedure manual had reported inconsistent retention of the training material. By creating asynchronous training modules, staff could rewatch videos to refresh their memory. This is key when there are delays between training and the launch of the program. Atkins (2004, 86) noted the difficulty for staff retention of training materials when delays occurred. The ability to rewatch training videos proved to be beneficial when training during a pandemic, and staff worked on a rotational basis. Staff could rewatch the videos prior to an in-library shift where they would be using Alma hands-on.

Learning together—and learning from each other—was a great benefit. The team-oriented learning modules, the UTL group sessions in Zoom and Teams, and the UTML team's review of the training materials and their adaptation to local use brought the team together, virtually, more often than other teams. This unexpectedly addressed concerns about staff working remotely during a pandemic related to staff wellness, isolation, and loneliness. The staff were reminded that this was new for everyone and were encouraged to share when they were feeling overwhelmed or frustrated. The result was that the UTML team now has a shared experience of learning together at a time when they could not be together in person.

Following the launch, one staffer remarked that the LSP launch was anticlimactic—that processing books live in Alma was much like how they had practiced it. This was attributed to how much staff had practiced in the test environment and how well prepared they were for the live environment. The staff's feedback on learning remotely was positive. They liked viewing the videos as a group. Staff members reported that they liked going through the workflow with the team and felt comfortable asking questions that they might not have asked in larger group settings. One staff member stated they "didn't feel stupid asking questions, it's just us, among friends." Learning from others in the AMA sessions was also helpful since others might be at a different stage and they could learn from their colleagues' experiences. The staff especially liked how the training videos could be rewatched before returning to in-library work, so they could refresh their memory.

CONCLUSION

The COVID-19 pandemic has changed the way many libraries operate. Migrating to a new library services platform and training staff on its use during the pandemic presented many challenges. While many staff had concerns about learning how to use the new system while working remotely, there were several unexpected benefits that stemmed from the asynchronous learning environment created by the functional teams and developed at the local level at UTML. Staff members could learn at their own pace, had opportunities to ask questions and learn from others, and had local supports to tailor their learning to the UTML environment. When the migration from Sirsi to Ex Libris Alma took place in January 2021, the UTML team was well prepared to work in the new system.

REFERENCES

Atkins, Stephanie S. 2004. "Circulation Training in an Integrated Library System: A Case Study at the University of Illinois at Urbana-Champaign Library." *Journal of Access Services* 1, no. 4: 77–87. https://doi.org/10.1300/J204v01n04_06.

Epps, Sharon K., Judith Kidd, Toni Negro, and Sheridan L. Sayles. 2016. "Rethinking Customer Service Training: A Curricular Solution to a Familiar Problem." *Journal of Access Services* 13, no. 3: 199–209. https://doi.org/10.1080/15367967.2016.1206476.

Kisby, Cynthia, and Marcus D. Kilman. 2008. "Improving Circulation Services through Staff Involvement." *Journal of Access Services* 5, no. 1–2: 103–12. https://doi.org/10.1080/15367960802198390.

McKenna, Julia. 2020. "So Many Students, So Little Time: Practical Student Worker Training in an Academic Library." *Journal of Access Services* 17, no. 1: 74–82. https://doi.org/10.1080/15367967.2020.1718505.

Michalak, Russell, and Monica D. T. Rysavy. 2018. "Online Onboarding: Library Workplace Training in a Trilingual Interactive Online Asynchronous Environment." In *Digital Workplace Learning*, edited by D. Ifenthaler, 291–306. Wilmington, DE: Springer International. https://doi.org/10.1007/978-3-319-46215-8_16.

University of Toronto Mississauga. n.d. "UTM Fact Sheet for 2021–2022." www.utm.utoronto.ca/about-us/fact-sheet.

Reinvention of Student Worker Training

A Positive Response and Outcome to Disruption

Leslie A. Engelson

WITH THE ELIMINATION OF STAFF LINES AND OTHER BUDGET-TIGHTENING measures, student workers are a necessity in academic libraries. Particularly in cataloging and other technical services departments, student workers provide the workforce to complete manual, repetitive, and routine tasks so that staff can focus on the complex and more advanced tasks. Employing student workers in cataloging departments can be challenging, however, because of the nature of both the work and the workers. Student workers are temporary, part-time employees who have little (if any) experience. They are usually working in the library strictly for the income involved, and not for career development. Many of the quickly learned tasks have now been automated, and what remains is the physical processing of materials and other activities that either require an understanding and application of international standards, or else are tedious, rote tasks. Moreover, a variety of software programs, including the library services platform (LSP), are often essential to use in order to accomplish these tasks.

The goal of cataloging department supervisors is to train student workers efficiently and effectively while ensuring quality, accuracy, and consistency in their output. While written procedures are important and online tutorials can be implemented, many of the tasks require one-on-one training. Communication with other cataloging staff about the student workers' training progress is essential. Even when an effective training program is in place, circumstances can sometimes disrupt that program. With a nimble and proactive response, however, that disruption can be a catalyst for bringing about positive change.

LITERATURE REVIEW

While much of the literature on training student workers in libraries from the past fifteen years has focused on public services positions, three articles do address training student workers in technical services (Chen 2008, Gainer and Mascaro 2012, and Martinez 2014).

At the Ohio State University Libraries, Chen (2008, 225) describes how the need for a "frequent but irregular" training cycle with a changing staff of ten student workers led to the development of an electronic, self-paced learning program for the practical aspects of cataloging work. While this courseware does not eliminate one-on-one instruction, it "reduces the repetition of training time and workload placed on a supervising librarian." It also "allows self-paced learning and is more convenient to use on the learner's side" (232).

Gainer and Mascaro (2012) detail the training provided to student workers for a project to create metadata for digitized images. The ten students who worked on this project were provided approximately forty hours of training each. This included one-on-one training with a metadata specialist, a metadata manual, and guides for searching and using the controlled vocabulary terms. Additionally, the metadata specialist reviewed each student's work until the error rate was at an acceptable level. The authors acknowledge that the training was time-consuming, but they concluded that it was worthwhile because it "result[ed] in less time correcting errors, a richer metadata record, and greater accessibility of information" (Gainer and Mascaro 2012, 20).

Martinez (2014) discusses how an awareness of cognitive load theory can impact the organization of technical services student workers' training. In addition to computer-based training, direct instruction, the use of task cards, and peer training, coaching and mentoring can also be used to develop highly motivated and successful student workers in technical services.

Many articles deal with training methods for library student workers (Connell and Mileham 2006, Jetton 2009, Farrell and Driver 2010, Leuzinger 2011, Power 2011, Manley and Holley 2014, Mestre and Lecrone 2015, Vassady, Arches, and Ackermann 2015, Becker-Redd, Lee, and Skelton 2018, Rex and Whelan 2019, and McKenna 2020), but the literature does not address how to

adapt a training program when the work environment is disrupted by a cata-
clysmic event such as a pandemic.

BACKGROUND

At Murray State University, a medium-sized public university located in Ken-
tucky, the labor that student workers provide in the Cataloging Department
enables the processing of physical materials and the completion of data integrity projects. The department's staffing consists of a metadata librarian who
manages the department, one paraprofessional staff member, and up to three
student workers.

When the university shut down the campus in response to the COVID-19
pandemic in March 2020, the manager of the Cataloging Department immediately petitioned to have at least one student worker continue working through
the end of spring semester and into the summer. All but a few public services
staff and the interim dean of libraries worked remotely for the next five
months, until the fall semester began.

The transition to working remotely was fairly seamless for the Cataloging
Department. The library's LSP is cloud based, and Google Docs are used for
file sharing. Trello, a free cloud-based project management platform, had
been implemented several months prior to the shutdown to organize a major
library-wide project, so it was easy to transition it to support the remote
workflow.

The student worker who continued working through the spring and summer was a recent hire with only about a month of on-site training before transitioning to a remote working environment.

SCAFFOLDED APPROACH TO TRAINING

Because of the complex nature of cataloging tasks, most of our training is done
one-on-one, along with some group training. For new student workers, the
department manager is intentional about scaffolding tasks so that the student
workers learn skills and concepts that build upon their previous knowledge.
This is based on cognitive load theory, which supports strategies of training
such as increasing difficulty (ID) and variable-priority training (VPT). ID and
VPT are suitable when people are at a novice stage in their learning and the

information is complex, so these strategies are ideal for student workers who have never worked in a library before. Scaffolded training based in ID and VPT strategies "gradually move[s] students from concrete learning based on personal experience to abstract, reflective learning that can then be applied to new contexts and situations" (Bates 2019, 315). This is important for developing student workers into employees who can make decisions based on their understanding of the concepts involved.

As student workers become proficient in a task, more challenging or complex elements are incorporated in subsequent training to build on what they already know and to grow their capabilities, with the training adjusted adaptively based on their performance. This approach to training continued in the remote working environment.

BATES' SECTIONS MODEL

During the pandemic, the department manager's primary concern was the staff's health and well-being. Once these were established, and both staff and student workers had the equipment and access they needed to work remotely, the department manager focused on facilitating communication and determining how to provide training. Good communication in any work environment is essential. It is no less important in a remote working environment, but is much more challenging to do logistically. Casual interactions are nonexistent, and interactions often must be planned and intentional. While it was important to establish reliable ways to provide feedback, hear and respond to questions, and determine priorities, it was crucial to find the best way to create opportunities for connecting consistently on an interpersonal level.

The department manager was always available via phone, text, and e-mail, but wanted to have a way for all Cataloging Department workers to communicate simultaneously, as well as use technology to facilitate training. Bates's SECTIONS model (2019) is a useful template for selecting technology for educational purposes, and was easy to adapt in order to determine which technology to use in this remote working environment. In brief, SECTIONS, as adapted, stands for:

> *Students*—the capabilities that student workers bring with them for using technology. Consider how much additional training is required, and whether access is easy on the devices used for work.

Ease of use—the quality of the interface design, its reliability to perform without crashing, its long-term stability, and the availability of support. Consider how intuitive, quick, and easy to navigate the tool is.

Costs—both time and money are to be considered. Some costs are fixed (onetime) and others are recurrent (ongoing). Categories of costs include development (the time to prepare the tool for use), delivery (the time spent interacting with the student worker while they used the tool), maintenance (the time spent updating content), and overhead (infrastructure, licensing, and bandwidth).

Teaching functions—the purpose of the tool as related to training and communication. This involves any constraints on what the tool was designed for versus how it would be used.

Interaction—the tool's ability to facilitate connection and communication with cataloging staff and student workers, as well as the ability to connect with materials.

Organizational issues—the tool's ability to conform to how the institution is organized, which involves a consideration of the technology already in place.

Networking—support for external connections to other tools such as Google Docs, websites, and YouTube videos.

Security—the tool's ability to accommodate institutional privacy and security policies; this involves online backups and security of content.

COMMUNICATION METHODS

As indicated previously, the infrastructure was already in place in the library to support a remote working environment. Many of the technology tools already in use were cloud based and incurred no additional monetary costs. Adapting Trello for communication and training purposes also provided a means to network with a variety of external tools, such as documentation and spreadsheets in Google Docs, tutorials from YouTube, and access to other tools via LibGuides.

Zoom, another free, cloud-based tool, was added to the repertoire of technology to replace in-person meetings. It was also used to record the tutorials that replaced some one-on-one training. All of these technological tools were low cost, easy to use and adapt for our purposes, and well suited to the organizational infrastructure of the university, and had the ability to conform to our institution's privacy and security policies.

The importance of connection and communication was immediately established through individually scheduled Zoom meetings with both staff and the student worker on a weekly basis. Every other week, the staff member would join the meeting with the student worker. More often than not, the agenda for these meetings was fairly loose. The primary purpose was support of one another by listening to concerns, celebrating accomplishments, and providing a moment of connection. Pets were introduced, artistic creations were admired, and laughter was exchanged through silly challenges. This was an incredible relationship-building and sustaining activity over those five isolating months. Of course, it also allowed opportunities for discussing work, asking and answering questions, establishing and communicating priorities, and determining areas for training as well.

Screen sharing with Zoom made it easy for the department manager to demonstrate a procedure and then watch the student worker walk through the procedure until both were confident it could be done independently. This was the next best thing to one-on-one training that could be done in a remote working environment.

ORGANIZING THE WORK BY USING TRELLO

Working remotely was a great opportunity to focus on much-needed database maintenance and integrity tasks that had previously been set aside because of other priorities. Trello was used to organize and monitor these tasks. Boards were created for both the staff member and the student worker. Both the staff member and the department manager created cards within the student worker's board as projects came up. (See figure 10.1.) Links were provided for procedures, spreadsheets, and training videos as appropriate.

When the student worker started a new task, she assigned herself to the card and dragged it to the Working On column. If it was a task she had not been trained on, the department manager sometimes created a tutorial, or else a live training was scheduled using Zoom for both. After a task was completed, the student worker dragged the card to the Complete column. A fun Trello feature was added to the Complete column so that when a card was moved to that column, digital confetti exploded across the screen.

At one point, the To Do column was split into two columns, one for online work that could be done remotely. These were the tasks that the student worker was expected to work on. The other column, To Do Onsite, was for work that required physical access to the library, and these tasks would wait until on-site working resumed. This method of keeping track of tasks is far better than trying to remember them or writing them on slips of paper that can be easily lost.

ORGANIZING THE TRAINING WITH CHECKLISTS

When the fall semester began, library staff returned to partial on-site work. To minimize potential risk, in addition to wearing masks and following social distancing protocols, the department manager and the cataloging staff member worked on-site on alternate days. None of the previous student workers returned, necessitating the hiring and training of two new student workers. This was an opportune time to incorporate the new ways the manager and staff member had used technology in the remote working environment into the on-site working environment.

Prior to remote working, the department manager had made a mental note of the tasks each student worker was trained on and whether they could perform that task independently or needed more review. This information was

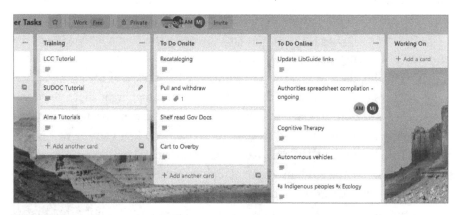

FIGURE 10.1
Cards on the student worker's task board in Trello

communicated to the cataloging staff person as needed. Upon return from remote working, however, with two new students to train and the cataloging staff working on-site on alternate days, staff members needed a more efficient way to communicate the training and capabilities of each student worker that was also confidential. A spreadsheet was shared between the cataloging staff person and the department manager that had a tab for each student worker which included a checklist of tasks. The tasks were grouped by type: Expectations, Orientation, Processing, Alma, Withdraw Shelf, Authorities, Mending, and so on, with more specific tasks listed under each category as appropriate. For instance, the Processing task is broken into eleven subtasks depending on how the resource was acquired, where it is going to be shelved, and the format. (See figure 10.2.) The subtasks are listed in order of their increasing complexity. Training begins with the first subtask in the list, and as the student worker develops competency in that subtask, they are then trained on the next subtask in the list, building new concepts onto the foundation they have already learned.

The checklist includes a column for the date when training started, the date the student worker became independent and their work no longer needed review, and a third column for notes and comments. Cataloging staff know what tasks a student worker has been trained on and can work on when they start their shift, whether the department manager is on-site or not. Notes are used to communicate if the student worker is doing particularly well with a task or if there are any areas that need additional training or closer monitoring. With this checklist, full-time cataloging staff are able to communicate and document student workers' progress and preferences easily and efficiently.

Both the cataloging staff person and the department manager generate a mixture of ongoing, periodic, and onetime tasks for student workers. Prior to utilizing Trello, there was no organized way to keep track of these tasks. Student workers had to ask one of the cataloging staff members if there were any projects to work on. It was challenging to know or remember what projects were waiting to be started and which project each student worker was working on. Trello changed all of that. Now, whenever either cataloging staff member has a task for the student workers to do, a card is created in Trello and is used in the same way as when the department was working entirely remotely.

The physical processing of new materials takes priority, but after that is complete, student workers check Trello for tasks available, attach their name

FIGURE 10.2
Part of training checklist

Processing				
	Shelf-ready	8/31/2020	9/8/2020	
	Taping spines	9/8/2020	9/10/2020	
	CPC	9/8/2020	9/10/2020	He caught on very quickly and proved to be quite capable.
	Main	9/8/2020	9/10/2020	
	Gov docs	9/10/2020	10/1/2020	
	Ref	10/13/2020	10/20/2020	Shown how to process books going to Info.
	AV	9/21/2020		
	Lobby (Games)			
	Scores			
	Laminating	9/14/2020	11/11/2020	He did great with his first lamination project.
	Limited retention	10/8/2020		Processed a couple books going to Info. Very good w/r/t following the directions on the retention slip.

to a card, and move it over to the Working On column. There is always something to do, and the student workers now have a measure of control over what they choose to work on. All cataloging staff members can know at any point who is working on a task and what stage of completion it is at.

Two additional columns were added to Trello to include documentation and training tutorials with the intention of moving the written procedures completely into Trello and creating additional video tutorials.

CONCLUSION

While the COVID-19 pandemic was a complete disruption and upheaval, the actions taken by the university in response to the pandemic precipitated the implementation and permanent adoption of workflows and tools that have facilitated the training and supervision of new student workers. The manager of the Cataloging Department took the opportunity to use technology to transform the way both training progress and task organization and workflow are monitored and communicated. This enables new student workers to more quickly become independent and highly functioning contributors to the progress and productivity of the department.

REFERENCES

Bates, A. W. (Tony). 2019. *Teaching in a Digital Age: Guidelines for Designing Teaching and Learning.* Vancouver, BC: Tony Bates Associates.

Becker-Redd, Kindra, Kirsten Lee, and Caroline Skelton. 2018. "Training Student Workers for Cross-Departmental Success in an Academic Library: A New Model." *Journal of Library Administration* 58: 153–65.

Chen, Sherab. 2008. "Empowering Student Assistants in the Cataloging Department through Innovative Training: The E-Learning Courseware for Basic Cataloging (ECBC) Project." *Cataloging & Classification Quarterly* 46, no. 2: 221–34.

Connell, Ruth Sara, and Patricia J. Mileham. 2006. "Student Assistant Training in a Small Academic Library." *Public Services Quarterly* 2, no. 2/3: 69–84.

Farrell, Sandy L. and Driver, Carol. 2010. "Tag, You're It: Hiring, Training, and Managing Student Assistants." *Community & Junior College Libraries* 16, no. 3: 185-191.

Gainer, Emily, and Michelle Mascaro. 2012. "Faster Digital Output: Using Student Workers to Create Metadata for a Grant Funded Project." *Provenance, Journal of the Society of Georgia Archivists* 31, no. 1: 8–28.

Jetton, Lora Lennertz. 2009. "Selecting and Using Technology for Student Training." *Technical Services Quarterly* 26, no. 1: 21–35.

Leuzinger, Julie. 2011. "Connect with Your Part-Time Library Staff: Using Learning Styles to Individualize Training." *Texas Library Journal* 87, no. 3: 78–80.

Manley, Laura, and Robert P. Holley. 2014. "Hiring and Training Work-Study Students: A Case Study." *College & Undergraduate Libraries* 21, no. 1: 76–89.

Martinez, Shan Lorraine. 2014. "Training Tech Services' Student Employees Well: Evidence-Based Training Techniques in Conjunction with Coaching and Mentoring Strategies." *Cataloging & Classification Quarterly* 52, no. 5: 551–61.

McKenna, Julia. 2020. "So Many Students, So Little Time: Practical Student Worker Training in an Academic Library." *Journal of Access Services* 17, no. 2: 74–82.

Mestre, Lori S., and Jessica M. Lecrone. 2015. "Elevating the Student Assistant: An Integrated Development Program for Student Library Assistants." *College & Undergraduate Libraries* 22: 1–20.

Power, June L. 2011. "Training 2.0—Library Assistants in the Age of Information." *Journal of Access Services* 8: 69–79.

Rex, Jared Andrew, and Jennifer L. A. Whelan. 2019. "The Undergraduate That Could: Crafting a Collaborative Student Training Program." *College & Undergraduate Libraries* 26, no. 1: 19–34.

Vassady, Lisa, Alyssa Arches, and Eric Ackermann. 2015. "READ-ing Our Way to Success: Using the READ Scale to Successfully Train Reference Student Assistants in the Referral Model." *Journal of Library Administration* 55, no. 7: 535–54.

Training Tech Services Using Concepts from Information Literacy Instruction

Jharina Pascual

IN TRADITIONAL MODELS OF MANAGEMENT AND ORGANIZATION FOR libraries, the training and delivery of public and technical services tend to be disparate tasks, requiring different skill sets. Given budgetary concerns, it is understandable that libraries focus their staffing and training in public-facing areas, with a corresponding deemphasis on the areas of acquisitions, cataloging, and other behind-the-scenes work. Library administrators have been encouraged in this regard by developments in service and content delivery from vendors, which promise more automation of routine tasks on the back end, as well as the instantaneous and aggregated delivery of scholarly content online or through interlibrary loan. All of this is designed to reduce the work for library employees to collect, deliver, and maintain relevant resources, which in turn is intended to allow for more attention on direct interactions with patrons.

The advanced networks for libraries' automated management and delivery systems have become increasingly granular and intricate, and therefore difficult to understand and implement; this is particularly acute given the growing demands for electronically available content. For academic libraries, the process and budgets required to purchase, maintain, and teach increasingly complex web-based resources has placed the demand on all staff to have some cursory knowledge of the systems, metadata, and algorithms used to manage and link these resources to patrons.

It can be useful for technical services supervisors and trainers to compare their role to that of reference and instruction librarians. The training and practice for understanding workflows within next-generation library systems should be like the instruction that patrons need to effectively use content online. While staff continue to benefit from ongoing guidance and procedures from supervisors, a complex and constantly changing metadata environment requires flexibility and problem-solving acuity to complete routine work, especially for those involved in the electronic resources workflow for libraries.

This chapter outlines theories and models of learning that are typically associated with formal instruction, particularly as discussed by Esther S. Grassian and Joan R. Kaplowitz in *Information Literacy Instruction: Theory and Practice* (2009). These models were applied both formally and informally for electronic resources staff training during a migration from one integrated library system, Millennium, to another, Alma. While staff can operate with more autonomy than students, the use of more structured methods of lecturing alongside ad hoc training seems to have produced positive results in terms of staff productivity, adaptability, and confidence in working with the new system.

DEVELOPING METHODS OF ELECTRONIC RESOURCES MANAGEMENT, TRAINING, AND COMMUNICATION

Research and retrospectives on electronic resource management in libraries tend to focus on the complexities of the skill sets required, as well as the ongoing life cycle in which, unlike print, the management of electronic content is never "completed." Instead, electronic resource staff and managers need continually updated knowledge, since library vendors are continually changing their modes of access, IT infrastructure, and/or budgeting and cost standards. This process was codified by Emery, Stone, and McCracken in their TERMS, or "techniques for electronic resource management" (2017). NASIG's (the North American Serials Interest Group's) "Core Competencies for Electronic Resources Librarians" attempts to define the areas of subject expertise needed to maintain this knowledge (Sutton et al. 2021). To manage electronic resources, librarians need to have theoretical and practical knowledge of the IT infrastructures and assessment methods that are specifically designed for online scholarly content, and they need to train and communicate the major workflows and timelines of e-resource access to other staff members.

In 2017, Carter and Traill focused a discussion of skill sets and techniques for e-resources management on the specific process of implementing and training staff in the Ex Libris Alma environment—an environment which incorporated previously separate aspects of resource management, such as the acquisitions, cataloging, and electronic resources modules, into one interface (Carter and Traill 2017). This study is notable because it also integrates the structured training of technical services staff for the public-facing interfaces, including how patrons encounter data from link resolvers, authentication protocols like proxies, and vendor-managed metadata. Electronic resources managers have also integrated methods from software development protocols such as the "agile" technique (Collins and Wilson 2018). In this approach, staff are trained to manage change and documentation within an iterative process of developing workflows, in an environment where testing and experimentation are constant.

CONTEXT

The University of California Irvine (UCI) is part of a consortium of the largest public research institutions in the state of California. Most of the online content for all the University of California (UC) campus libraries is licensed, acquired, and managed by the administration and staff of the California Digital Library (CDL) consortium. Although the UC campuses share this content through CDL-managed platforms and have access to a union catalog, prior to July 2021 each of the UC campuses maintained its own online public access catalog (OPAC) and integrated library system (ILS). As of July 2021, however, the CDL consortium's entire membership has merged their OPACs and ILS data into one instance of Primo and Alma.

The UCI Libraries' electronic resources unit (ER unit) is part of the Acquisitions Department, which operates with two librarian positions (the electronic resources acquisitions librarian and the head of acquisitions) and between nine and twelve staff members. There are four librarian positions and similar numbers of staff in the Cataloging Department.

The ER unit, supervised by the electronic resources acquisitions librarian (ERAL), is responsible for the licensing, acquisition, implementation, and maintenance of all locally purchased electronic resources. The ER unit's responsibilities include communicating information about vendors and electronic resources to library- and campus-level information technology units, collection development librarians, reference staff, and of course, patrons. Even though ER unit staff are not responsible for consortium-managed content, they are nevertheless asked to research, communicate, and troubleshoot access to those resources.

The ER unit shares many workflows with the Cataloging Department, which prepares electronic resource records for the OPAC after the ER unit completes activation of the resource. The ER unit and the Cataloging Department members who work with electronic resources regularly come together to address new library acquisitions, projects, and policies that may impact current workflows, and to discuss possible efficiencies.

Previously, the UCI Libraries used iii's Millennium ILS, which like most systems was built around the management and discovery of print-based resources. The UCI Libraries' workflows derived specifically from using this system; it was while using this system that the UCI Libraries began to answer the growing demand for electronic resources, and the offerings from vendors became more sophisticated and expensive. However, reference and bibliographic instruction were still centered on searching for mainly print resources within the OPAC and showing title-level metadata. Many bibliographic discovery and access concerns were addressed through title-level records in the local OPAC.

MENTAL MODELS

It is important to establish this context because it provides the mental models with which the UCI Libraries staff initially approached the first local migration to Alma and Primo. Grassian and Kaplowitz, in *Information Literacy Instruction*, define a mental model as "a miniature of a real-world object or system . . . and . . . a theory that generates predictions" (2009, 73). Despite working with electronic content that was accessed in ways not limited to a title-level MARC record, the ER unit conceived of its work within these mental models.

These models can impede learning how to work with electronic resources in Alma and Primo, which apply web-scale discovery, integrating resources from a variety of sources into the library catalog to mimic searches on web browsers (Breeding 2007). This kind of user experience is considerably different from previous iterations of the catalog: the public interface is no longer reliably a reflection of records, pages, and other content directly produced and/or collected by library staff at the home institution. This has tended to produce a level of discomfort and distrust of web-scale discovery technology among librarians immediately after a system migration (Renaville, Richelle, and Thirion 2013).

Nevertheless, research has demonstrated that web-scale discovery has changed how research is taught and performed, given the volume of online resources and the increasing complexity of faceting; it follows that library staff have also had to change the ways in which they manage these resources (Richardson 2013). The ER unit staff's transition from the mental models of the print-centric Millennium ILS to the electronic resource-intensive Alma-Primo began by trying to analogize their previous mental models of the library catalog to the heuristics of the Alma and Primo database(s) (Grassian and Kaplowitz 2009, 73–77).

Comparing the conceptual frameworks of Millennium and Alma-Primo enabled staff members to recognize routine functions in the new system by using the framework with which they already felt comfortable.

THE PRESENTATION-APPLICATION-FEEDBACK MODEL: PRESENTATION

There are a few models discussed by Grassian and Kaplowitz that incorporate different learning theories into practice, but the ERAL's training of the staff coincided with a structure called the "presentation-application-feedback model," or PAF (2009, 57). Within this model, the ER unit staff began the transition prior to the go-live date with Alma ILS, with the ERAL presenting the overarching metadata and workflow structures of Alma by comparing it to their existing knowledge of similar structures in Millennium.

The primary emphasis during training was to discuss Millennium's and Alma's contrasting approaches to print and electronic formats. Unlike Millennium, Alma separates workflows between print and electronic acquisitions and management. The ER unit discussed the different ways in which these formats are documented inside the system. The ERAL's presentations contrasted Millennium's generic bibliographic record with Alma's portfolio model. Alma differentiates physical items in holdings records from electronic URLs, which are stored in records called portfolios. The ERAL also discussed how creating purchase order records of a particular type in Alma created these differentiated holdings. The ERAL used the team's knowledge of the consortium's link resolver, SFX, to discuss the different types of electronic resource holdings (or inventory) in Alma. Finally, the ERAL emphasized the importance of understanding what we wanted to find and create before creating an order in the ILS because many of the functional fixed fields would automatically trigger jobs and workflows to run a certain way in the ILS.

The ERAL also discussed the FRBRized metadata structures inside Alma, in which one bibliographic record could be associated with a variety of items, including both print and online ones. Electronic metadata could be connected to a variety of levels of presentation—not just at the title-level record, but also at the more granular levels of chapters, articles, and encyclopedia entries, depending on the type of resource. These structures also affect the OPAC and the ER unit's troubleshooting.

THE PRESENTATION-APPLICATION-FEEDBACK MODEL: APPLICATION AND THEORIES OF LEARNING

Very few of these major contrasts would become salient until the ER staff actually had direct experience searching, creating, and troubleshooting records within Alma and Primo. The "application" portion of the PAF model combines elements of several major teaching and learning theories.

The "cognitive model" of psychology posits that people learn through a holistic approach to training, applying complex ideas to concrete situations, recognizing patterns, and constructing their own meanings and ideas out of recognizing those patterns. Per Grassian and Kaplowitz, it is the teacher's role to present ideas to facilitate these connections, but this work is an iterative process (2009, 35).

The cognitive model as it was deployed in the ERAL's management and training consisted of:

- Presentations on the larger workflows and metadata structures in Alma and Primo
- Working with draft procedures of routine workflows in those systems

- Regular meetings and check-ins with ER unit staff to discuss the work
- Regular staff involvement in decision-making about policies and procedures
- Providing time for staff feedback and informal assessment of their work and policies in general

The "discovery" method of cognitive psychology resulted in a more communal method of learning and management of the unit's work (Grassian and Kaplowitz 2009, 34–36). While ER unit staff began with draft procedures initially written by the ERAL, the meetings and check-ins provided opportunities for them to recommend changes. Regular staff involvement with decisions about their own assignments not only reinforced the concepts from the presentations, but also enabled them to reflect on their own learning processes and their engagement with the larger purpose of their work. This fostered confidence in their own knowledge and critical thinking skills when performing work that required more decision-making and flexibility outside of routine procedures. The manager must allow the learning and the work to take place at the pace of individual staff members, as well as let go of some control over training structure, content, and materials.

The "behaviorist" model of psychology proposes that learning takes place through hands-on experience; this theory aligns with the "application" portion of the presentation-application-feedback model. Within this learning theory, the instructor provides an environment in which students learn ideas or procedures through a process of trial and error (Grassian and Kaplowitz 2009, 29–30), while the instructor provides specific examples so that complex tasks are segmented, practiced, and eventually mastered by students.

The behaviorist model as it was deployed in the ERAL's management and training consisted of:

- Working directly with staff as they began to use draft procedures of routine workflows, and making corrections as needed
- Providing concrete examples of ILS record creation, searching, and troubleshooting in real time in order to model correct procedures, as well as in-context decision-making
- Breaking whole workflows down into specific tasks and practicing them with staff repeatedly within different troubleshooting scenarios

The elements of active learning and chunking tasks are not only effective for students, but also seem helpful for staff in managing technological or structural changes in their work. ER unit staff are encouraged to work hands-on but, more importantly, to make mistakes as they do so, with guidance and corrections when necessary from the ERAL. This also encourages staff to look at large, potentially problematic projects in more manageable chunks, which tends to mitigate their anxiety about electronic resource troubleshooting.

THE PRESENTATION-APPLICATION-FEEDBACK MODEL: FEEDBACK

Both the cognitive and behaviorist models of learning are dependent upon feedback from the learner. This happens in the process of presenting and applying procedures; however, it is important for instructors to create consistent space for discussing how their staff or students are experiencing the work, and to develop the unit's internal processes for integrating that feedback into concrete changes. In the ER unit, these processes include:

- Regularly scheduled meetings to discuss whether procedures are current or out-of-date (this was a quarterly process modeled by the UCI Libraries' Cataloging Department that was later adopted by the ER unit)
- Quarterly meetings between members of the Cataloging and ER units assigned to work with electronic resources in order to discuss new acquisitions, new procedures, assessment of current workflows, and other topics relevant to online resources
- Weekly meetings with the entire ER unit staff, as well as individual staff meetings as needed, to discuss specific projects or problems with routine work or perform ad hoc training and reinforcement of concepts
- Providing time for changes to be absorbed by the staff

Overall, this approach to training staff can be collected under the umbrella of "learner-centered teaching," which mandates that an environment for teaching be constructed to discover and amplify individual learners' specific needs. The learners are thus able to develop their own connections to ideas, practice at their own pace, and identify and use the methods and environments in which they are best able to perform work (Grassian and Kaplowitz 2009, 37-39). It is important for the manager to create relationships between unit and department members so that these ideas, methods, and environments are communicated and implemented wherever possible.

AD HOC ASSESSMENT

Admittedly, the foregoing approach may not seem the most efficient or easy way to teach and implement new workflows, but within the context of training for and implementing the use of Alma and Primo, it has produced positive productivity results and constructive methods of thinking about training more generally within the complex environment of library electronic resources at UC Irvine. The ERAL has informally observed improvement and/or received constructive comments from ER unit staff:

- Staff have said (via informal comments and a survey) that they found the formal presentations of the structures and metadata in Alma to be helpful alongside practicing the new workflows (Pascual and Wallbank 2021).
- Staff find it helpful to meet weekly and walk through troubleshooting scenarios.
- Staff find it helpful to regularly discuss and change workflows not only to reinforce and clarify their understanding of them, but to provide feedback and suggest avenues for improvement.
- Staff find it helpful to continually analogize their new workflows in Alma and Primo using concepts from their procedures in Millennium.
- Staff feedback about training methods and their effectiveness has provided the ERAL with an opportunity to develop different methods of delivering information.
- Staff are now able to ask relevant questions and independently make decisions to complete their work outside of standard procedures.
- Staff can draft new step-by-step procedures for electronic resource workflows in Alma after one or two demonstrations.
- Staff can identify major areas of missing training and/or information as needed and follow up with the ERAL accordingly.
- Staff have been able to complete more routine work with less guidance.
- Individual staff members can identify general areas of troubleshooting electronic resources more effectively: vendor access, ILS metadata,

Primo user interface issues, consortium access issues, and link resolver problems.

- Staff have become adaptable to frequent adjustments in procedure necessitated by changes to metadata structures in Alma, Primo, and other databases.
- The ERAL has introduced non-routine, project-based work without extant procedures to staff, such as exploring and discussing the metadata produced by Alma's Community Zone Update Task Lists, DARA, and cleaning up migrated Millennium records.
- Staff can start project-based work with minimal guidance and are able to collaborate in the ongoing development of those projects.
- The ERAL has integrated the use of non-ILS technology (such as wiki pages for writing procedures, or Microsoft Teams for communication and file management) after the staff exhibited more confidence in executing routine procedures and troubleshooting in Alma, Primo, and vendor/publisher websites, in order to mitigate anxiety about new technology or interfaces (Grassian and Kaplowitz 2009, 69–71).

One area that has consistently needed improvement for the entire ER unit, including the librarian, is the provision of time to reflect on changes to these systems and on procedures and policies at large, a common problem for anyone who must provide timely service. Prioritizing a "getting it done" attitude over intentional reflection and scaffolding of knowledge can result in major gaps in knowledge that will become more evident when more complex tasks arise (Grassian and Kaplowitz 2009, 54). The ERAL has noted that when time is not taken to explain and reflect, the same problems reappear and eventually become a bottleneck in the work. This also results in negligent communication about changes in policy, which results in out-of-date procedures and more retroactive clean-up.

In the process of training people to work with electronic resources, managers should think medium- and long-term about the advantages and disadvantages of delaying more structured and intentional training and teaching practices within their units and departments. The ILS, publisher sites, link resolvers, and other technology for managing and distributing electronic resources are continually updated, and to keep current requires that workers have a different modality than the rote practice of certain workflows and a siloed understanding of metadata.

This advice applies to anyone who may be involved in the process of implementing, maintaining, and troubleshooting these environments. Moreover, many of the techniques discussed in this chapter could be applied to everyone in a library environment who is providing public services related to electronic resources.

CONCLUSION

In their discussion of the agile approach to technical services, Collins and Wilson note that "libraries are often very passive institutions. We wait for innovations to evolve and then join the fray. Technical service operations are in the midst of tremendous change. The skills staff have obtained from years of data and metadata work are critical for creating the next iteration of access and discovery services. For most of us there is no clear path. It may not even be possible to know an exact path to take to create innovative technical services work" (2018, 11). The theories and methods outlined in this chapter attempt to reintroduce concepts of reference and instruction and direct them toward ourselves. When library managers and staff are expected to develop, guide, scaffold, and continually reinforce their critical thinking about information resources, they can also see their own training as a method of developing information literacy. Within this model, one should not expect a rote execution of specific steps, but an evolving and iterative process that supports the entire library's ability to deliver timely and relevant public services in an ever-expanding, increasingly complex information landscape.

REFERENCES

Breeding, Marshall. 2007. "Next-Generation Library Catalogs: Chapter 1 Introduction." *Library Technology Reports*, July/August. https://librarytechnology.org/document/18344.

Carter, Sunshine, and Stacie Traill. 2017. "Essential Skills and Knowledge for Troubleshooting E-Resources Access Issues in a Web-Scale Discovery Environment." *Journal of Electronic Resources Librarianship* 29, no. 1: 1–15. https://doi.org/10.1080/1941126X.2017.1270096.

Collins, Maria, and Kristen Wilson. 2018. "An Agile Approach to Technical Services." *Serials Librarian* 74, no. 1–4: 9–18. https://doi.org/10.1080/03615 26X.2018.1443652.

Emery, Jill, Graham Stone, and Peter McCracken. 2017. "TERMS ver2.0 Introduction, March 24." https://library.hud.ac.uk/archive/projects/terms/terms-ver2-0-introduction/.

Grassian, Esther S., and Joan R. Kaplowitz. 2009. *Information Literacy Instruction: Theory and Practice.* 2nd edition. New York: Neal-Schuman.

Hulseberg, Anna. 2016. "Technical Communicator: A New Model for the Electronic Resources Librarian?" *Journal of Electronic Resources Librarianship* 28, no. 2: 84–92. https://doi.org/10.1080/1941126X.2016.1164555.

Morales, Jessica M., and Christina A. Beis. 2021. "Communication across the Electronic Resources Lifecycle: A Survey of Academic Libraries." *Journal of Electronic Resources Librarianship* 33, no. 2: 75–91. https://doi.org/10.1080/1941 126X.2021.1913841.

Pascual, Jharina, and Sarah Wallbank. 2021. "Analyzing Workflows and Improving Communication across Departments: A Quick and Simple Project Using Rapid Contextual Design." *Serials Librarian* 80, no. 1–4: 11–18. doi: 10.1080/0361526X.2021.1877996.

Rathmel, Angela, Liisa Mobley, Buddy Pennington, and Adam Chandler. 2015. "Tools, Techniques, and Training: Results of an E-Resources Troubleshooting Survey." *Journal of Electronic Resources Librarianship* 27, no. 2: 88–107. https://doi.org/10.1080/1941126X.2015.1029398.

Renaville, François, Laurence Richelle, and Paul Thirion. 2013. "'Where Are My Marc Records?' Librarians' Perception of Discovery Tools." IGeLU 2013 Conference, Berlin. http://dx.doi.org/10.13140/RG.2.1.5096.2087.

Richardson, Hillary A. H. 2013. "Revelations from the Literature." *Computers in Libraries,* May. www.infotoday.com/cilmag/may13/Richardson--How-Web -Scale-Discovery-Has-Already-Changed-Us.shtml.

Sutton, Sarah, Eugenia Beh, Steve Black, Clint Chamberlain, Susan Davis, Katy Ginanni, Selden Lamoureux, Sanjeet Mann, Cynthia Porter, and Taryn Resnick. 2021. "Core Competencies for E-Resources Librarians." NASIG 2021. www.nasig.org/Competencies-Eresources.

UCI Libraries. 2021. "Facts and Figures." www.lib.uci.edu/facts-and-figures.

University of California Irvine. 2021. "University Facts." www.uci.edu/docs/UCI21-facts-figures-final.pdf.

Reactive and Proactive Approaches in the Training Program for the University of Nevada, Las Vegas Acquisitions Unit

Jennifer R. Culley

THE UNIVERSITY OF NEVADA, LAS VEGAS (UNLV) IS A PUBLIC DOCTORAL-granting institution with approximately 31,000 students. University Libraries are made up of five libraries: the Architectural Studies Library, Health Sciences Library, Lied Library (the main library), Music Library, and the Teacher Development & Resource Library.

The Acquisitions unit in Lied Library is composed of two librarians, two classified staff, and two student workers. A restructuring consolidated all acquisitions functions—such as ordering physical and electronic resources, receiving physical resources, electronic resource activating, electronic resource troubleshooting, physical processing, invoice processing, and cancellations of continuing resources—into one unit. The newly combined unit currently performs these duties for all five of the university's libraries.

Jennifer was hired as lead acquisitions librarian for the newly combined unit. It was necessary at the time for her to learn her job and the jobs of her direct reports. She asked them to train her on what they do. This helped her learn, showed interest in what they do, and informed her if they were comfortable and confident in the work they had been doing. Jennifer reviewed and asked questions about the training manuals or procedures that they, or their students, were currently using. In addition to training, this was also a fact-finding mission to assess the potential changes that needed to be made in the acquisitions area, and the potential training needs of staff and students.

ON-THE-JOB TRAINING

Jennifer used her previous library experience as a case study for some of the training, as many of the tasks currently performed were ones she had carried out in previous positions. The training at UNLV has all been practical and directly job related. Unofficially, her method for training follows that of William J. Rothwell and H. C. Kazanas (2004). Their strategy includes finding the benefits of on-the-job training; identifying goals; ensuring sound management and consistent results; analyzing the work, workers, and workplace to fit the training to the job; preparing the training plan; and evaluating results.

The benefit of on-the-job training for new staff or students is that they can learn the skills their job requires without necessarily having acquisitions experience. It is helpful for them to come into the job with certain traits, however, including openness to new ideas, attention to detail, and the ability to follow directions. Many of these skills can be seen in their past work experience or in the thoroughness of their application materials. The benefit of training on the job is that all staff and students are trained with the exact same information to preserve continuity in the standard work. It is not easy to train a diverse group of people in faculty, staff, and student positions while also being a new employee.

After evaluating the training and procedures she had received from the staff, Jennifer was able to identify goals for future training or retraining, including any changes needed to streamline workflows. For example, she implemented a new type of security strip and trained staff and students in its use, thereby reducing placement errors and increasing efficiency. Another example was a vendor report that was previously saved in two formats, in at least three locations, which seemed redundant and unnecessary. Jennifer updated the procedures to save the report in one format in one location. Training for this was minimal and consisted mostly of edits to the current procedures document.

In addition to streamlining and improving workflows, training was required for new duties transferred to the unit, which included receiving and processing print standing orders, print journals, newspapers and microfilm, and electronic continuing resources invoice processing. Aligning these new duties helped streamline the processes and cut down on opportunities for mistakes or discrepancies, such as the date entered when receiving materials. In one receiving workflow, the date the item entered the unit was used; while in another workflow, the date the item was actually received in the system was used. While both have their merits, the decision was made to enter the date the item was received in the system. Training or retraining was also necessary because Jennifer implemented the cross-training of staff and students. Some staff had been cross-trained, but it had been some time since the initial training. Peer-to-peer training helped reduce the time commitment needed for Jennifer to train people, and it gave the staff more experience in training and reviewing the procedures.

TRAINING WITH STANDARD WORK

The Acquisitions unit creates written documentation for all procedures and tasks; this standard work is also used for training, which ensures sound management and consistent results with each person trained. The documentation consists of print and electronic procedures, with photos or screenshots to serve as a visual guide for the processing of materials. (See figure 12.1 for staff procedures on creating new records in the library system. Figure 12.2 shows a brief procedure used for receiving materials that cost more than $500.)

The written procedures are grouped together for students, but for staff with more complex jobs, they are broken down into documents that are for their major job responsibilities and tasks.

Student Procedures Examples:
- Labeling books
- Unpacking boxes
- Processing the leisure reading collection

Staff Procedures Examples:
- Ordering materials in our main vendor's system
- Ordering materials outside of the main vendor
- Processing approval orders
- Creating bibliographic and order records
- Receiving ordered materials
- Receiving and processing of print journals and standing orders
- Invoice processing

Records Creation for Print Materials in Alma

1. Log in to Alma: https://unlv.alma.exlibrisgroup.com. The "Welcome, [Your Name Here]" screen appears.

2. From the left side bar, click on Resources(1), then click on Open Metadata Editor(2).

FIGURE 12.1
Staff procedure for creating new records in Alma

**RECEIVING EXPENSIVE SPECIAL COLLECTIONS ITEMS—
$500 OR MORE & EXCEPTION**

1. After unpacking item(s), print out a copy of the brief bibliographic record and place inside/with the item.
2. Next, invoice and receive the item.
3. Finally, hand deliver the item to the Specialized Collections Catalog Librarian. If unavailable give to the Lead Acquisitions Librarian. Do not leave these items unattended on a cart.

Exception: Special Collections materials are sometimes ordered/purchased directly by the Head of Special Collections. This sometimes results in items shipped to, or given to, the Head of Special Collections instead of the Acquisitions unit. These items must be seen in person by a staff member in the Acquisitions unit prior to receiving in the system. This can be done by either requesting them to be delivered to the Acquisitions unit, when possible, or by an Acquisitions unit staff member going to Special Collections to view the item.

FIGURE 12.2
Staff procedure for receiving expensive items

All staff members completed web tutorials for various processes in Alma, the library services platform (LSP), and the staff who handle physical processing received hands-on training. Staff who process materials electronically participated in either in-person or virtual demonstrations of the steps for processing invoices. In some cases, Jennifer did quality checking to ensure that all processes were followed. She briefly checked the physical processing of print materials by both staff and students. As part of her normal workflow, she approves invoices and verifies that they are correct in the financial system and in Alma.

As not all people learn the same way, the Acquisitions unit employs various tools and a variety of methods in training. Students receive hands-on training, primarily using procedures that include screenshots or other images as necessary. The images show application techniques for security strips, call number and property stamping placement, and so on. The unit also created guides to help aid in the proper placement of labels on books. The student procedures manual is currently a physical book but is transitioning to online.

IDENTIFYING TRAINING NEEDS AND OPPORTUNITIES FOR TRAINING

When analyzing training needs, it became clear that the biggest and immediate need was training for newly assigned duties such as invoice processing and the receiving and processing of print journals, standing orders, newspapers, and microfilm. When taking on these new duties, Jennifer conducted several sessions of in-person training for acquisitions staff, which offered several benefits. First, it ensured that Jennifer knew what tasks they were performing and how these would impact the workflow. Second, Jennifer could establish herself as a backup in case it was necessary for her to fill in. To help the staff learn more about the LSP, she sent Alma training videos to them. She also regularly sends the staff monthly LSP updates to ensure they know what new features are coming, which could be an opportunity for additional training on new features or upgrades.

Some of the hands-on training changed slightly due to the COVID-19 pandemic. As everyone in the unit was working all or mostly from home, virtual training through meeting systems such as Google Meet covered tasks that could be performed online, such as database maintenance in the LSP and invoice processing. The virtual training used screen sharing to walk through the processing steps in the financial system as these were being completed on an invoice. This helped staff more clearly see the steps and ask questions. It also brought to light several staff access issues that had impeded processing; Jennifer worked with the financial system administrators to fix these issues as they appeared. Jennifer makes herself available to answer questions, particularly to ensure that staff members understand how their work fits in the overall acquisitions process, which improves learning retention.

In addition to searching for training opportunities, Jennifer asks staff about their own training needs or if they have ideas for improvements. This helps staff feel engaged in the decision-making process for updates to workflows or procedures, potentially making their job easier or tasks quicker. Jennifer's questions to staff include: "What tasks do you feel you need more training on?" "What tasks/duties do you feel, even with training, that you still don't fully understand or feel comfortable with?" "After training, are there tasks that you feel could be done a better way?" Answers to these questions have ranged from increased training in the Analytics section of Alma to retraining on tasks that an employee had to assist with after a retirement, when the unit was short staffed.

Another proactive approach was to review workflows and procedures again as Jennifer became more comfortable with how the unit was doing things. This made it easier to spot problems such as multiple people doing a similar duty, but in another department. For example, staff in both the Acquisitions unit and in Special Collections receive print journals. The quantity of these is low enough to be seamlessly integrated into the workflow of Acquisitions, saving staff time in Special Collections and adding minimal work for the Acquisitions student employee.

PROACTIVE VS. REACTIVE

The approach to training has been both proactive and reactive as prompted by the situation. Proactive training is used for new workflows or new systems that the unit is transitioning to, particularly as new ways to do things better and more efficiently appear in the literature. When something is found that will be better than the current methods, the team makes the change and then trains everyone in the Acquisitions unit who will be impacted by the change. Two examples are the switch from a self-inking stamp that caused messy stamping to a fixed stamp that made a cleaner print; and a cardboard guide to help with more accurate label placement on books that was created for the student employees. Reminder retraining is a proactive method to refresh everyone on procedures over time.

Reactive training occurs for both work quality issues and new tasks in the Acquisitions unit. The unit sets certain quality standards, and monitors complaints about the processing of items and questions from staff. Jennifer began by investigating where a problem occurred and then assessed the relevant procedures again. If only one employee or student is struggling with quality-of-work issues, their retraining is done one-on-one. One librarian and both staff have worked at UNLV for over twenty years and have a good understanding of their job duties and procedures, although mistakes do happen. However, student turnover tends to be frequent, and each new student requires training. Students are less invested in a job they know to be temporary and part time when their primary focus is on their courses, so retraining and reminders are more frequent with this group.

It is good to have a plan for training and retraining, but ensuring buy-in requires giving personnel advanced notice of new tasks and trainings with opportunities to ask questions about it, as well as clearly explaining what the staff will be learning and why. Morale is important when training, especially around quality issues of standard work tasks. Managers should prepare for pushback and working through "killer" comments such as: "That's not my job. [This is] a waste of time. [This task is] too slow. Yes, but . . ." (Nilson 1994, 21), or that perennial favorite, "But this is how we've always done things." Transparency and talking through the changes and why changes are occurring can help staff understand better and get on board more easily. When staff do a good job, it is important to thank them, which can blunt any negative associations with retraining. "Remember: 'Thank you' is a phrase most people can never hear often enough" ("Morale Boosters" 2008, 13).

A participative management style can help with the staff's expectations and attitudes toward training and learning new skills. When the manager participates in training with staff and invests her time in learning the same skills, staff are more open and willing to train for new skills. They know that their manager will help them through the process. In addition, training alongside staff helps a manager evaluate the workload and work quality so that her expectations are realistic and consistent with the knowledge and training that the staff have. Showing appreciation for their willing participation and being accommodating can improve the staff's attitudes when going through change.

TRAINING FOLLOW-UP

There is always follow-up after training or retraining to ensure that all the procedures and workflows are understood with no problems, and to make any necessary updates to procedures that were identified during training or to reflect new processes. Also, Jennifer makes sure that all training documents and procedures are up-to-date each time they are used and that everyone is using the same version. Managers may assume that instructions will be easy to follow, yet they often discover that staff don't have access to all areas of the library systems platform or don't understand the terminology used in the procedure documents. Moreover, staff members aren't always willing to say that they don't understand, so asking is important. It is crucial to ensure that all staff have the access and tools they need to do their job properly.

Trainers should ask for feedback about the training and analyze the results of the training. Was it successful? Does the training or any of the training documents need to be adjusted? Was the training too short or too long? Should it have been spread out to avoid staff losing interest, or to maintain a manageable cognitive load? Trainers can also ask: "What things have you been trained on that you still don't feel comfortable with? Now that we have done the training you asked for, do you have a better understanding of this task? Do you still have questions?"

In addition to questions, managers can assess quality control on the tasks that were retrained. Is the quality better or are there still mistakes? Can the staff member who may be making mistakes be tracked to items so that they can receive further training? Reactive training will continue to be performed as needed, but Jennifer will continue to search the literature for new ways to do things and check in with staff members to see if they have ideas. Going forward, she plans to incorporate a yearly refresher of tasks, particularly physical processing.

CONCLUSION

Trainers, managers, and supervisors at other libraries can apply these techniques to their own technical service departments and create a training plan. Successful training programs start with a training plan, including what training is needed and why it's needed. It is important to have training documents and procedures ready prior to training, to organize the training presentation for efficiency, and to offer a variety of learning methods. Those who perform the training should be transparent about the why of training. Staff should be surveyed to ensure that the training has been understood, and they should be encouraged to ask questions. Anyone who does training should be flexible to changes. The whole point of some of the training is a result of changes in workflow, so the training must remain flexible too. Trainers need to be prepared to repeat steps multiple times. Trainers and managers should be open to criticism on their training techniques, documents, or document presentation, and on their explanations for why training is needed.

Training with staff is never a one-and-done occurrence. There are always changes in processes, software, or quality issues that require refreshers. It is also important for supervisors to keep training themselves. It is easy to forget all the tiny details of the work that staff are doing. Retraining on tasks every now and then will help make managers better. Staff will see managers involved in the work that they themselves do, and anything new in the field that could make tasks more efficient will be easier to identify if managers are familiar with those tasks. After training is complete, Jennifer will continue to quality-check periodically to ensure that there is no additional training needed. In theory, with greater proactive training, there should be less reactive training.

REFERENCES

"Morale Boosters for Tough Times—or Any Time." 2008. *HR Focus* 85, no. 9: 13.

Nilson, Carolyn D. 1994. *Peer Training: Improved Performance One by One*. Englewood Cliffs, NJ: Prentice Hall.

Rothwell, William J., and H. C. Kazanas. 2004. *Improving On-the-Job Training: How to Establish and Operate a Comprehensive OJT Program*. 2nd edition. San Francisco: Pfeiffer.

Technical Services Staff Training and Documentation during and after a Transition from Voyager to Alma

Daricus Larry

IN JUNE 2015, THE UNIVERSITY SYSTEM OF GEORGIA (USG) CHOSE EX Libris's Alma as a new library management system (LMS) to replace Voyager. Georgia Southern University was selected as one of three vanguard schools to test the new system and develop workflows and documentation to ease the transition for the other schools in the consortium. During the migration, Georgia Southern's primary focus was on replicating its current workflows in the new system, so that staff could hit the ground running by having a basic understanding of how to maneuver around the system. Georgia Southern also wanted staff to avoid having to continuously reference hard-to-follow and complex documentation from the Ex Libris Knowledge Center. Primary training goals were to identify where their work fell within the new workflow chain, encourage group input into the overall workflow, cross-train to enable others to step into other parts of the workflow, write accurate and easy-to-follow documentation, and finally to centralize that documentation in a location accessible to all. This chapter breaks down the process of how Collection and Resource Services accomplished these goals before and after the migration to Alma, and before and after the merger with Armstrong State University.

BACKGROUND

In July 2015, USG signed a contract with Ex Libris, solidifying their commitment to migrating their system to a next-generation library services platform, Alma. The University System of Georgia encompasses twenty-six higher education institutions, including four research universities, four comprehensive universities, nine state universities, and nine state colleges. To facilitate the transfer to Alma and enable the USG Libraries to get a jumpstart on creating documentation for staff training, three schools were selected as vanguard institutions: the University of Georgia, Georgia Southern University, and Valdosta State University. These vanguard universities had early access to a sandbox environment, pre-loaded with a sample of their data, to begin the process. At the Zach S. Henderson Library at Georgia Southern University, the Collection and Resource Services (CRS) and the Systems Department heads spearheaded the migration from Voyager to Alma for Georgia Southern.

Collection and Resource Services contained four internal interconnected units, which maintained different aspects of technical services: Cataloging and Metadata, Continuing Resources, Institutional Repository Services, and Special Collections. The department employed six librarians, each leading their own internal section with support staff. This case study focuses on staff training efforts, specifically those of the Cataloging and Metadata and Continuing Resources sections, during the following three phases:

Phase 1: Pre-migration training and documentation
Phase 2: Post-migration training and documentation
Phase 3: Pre- and post-merger training and documentation

Phase 1: Pre-Migration Documentation and Training

As a vanguard institution, Georgia Southern's early access to Alma allowed it to develop new workflows that could then be used by the central consortial committees to train all the member institutions. The leadership of Collection and Resource Services had two main goals for training their staff and developing workflows: educate and replicate. While Ex Libris did not offer formal training for using Alma, other than at the USG level, they did have an extensive set of instructional videos and the Ex Libris Knowledge Center, an encyclopedic information repository that houses preestablished workflows and tutorials. However, the Ex Libris Knowledge Center was not recommended as something that staff should navigate alone, as it was complex and could easily overwhelm those who were already having trouble adjusting.

CRS management decided to take advantage of the video tutorials as a team-building exercise that would allow staff to learn about Alma in a collaborative environment. Staff were assigned to a group based on their internal CRS unit or if tutorials had potential relevance to their work. While these group sessions allowed staff to see only static examples, the exercise alleviated some of the tension and apprehension that had built up regarding moving to a new LMS. The group sessions also gave the department management an opportunity to take note of questions that could be passed along to Ex Libris. The CRS leadership team attended a regularly scheduled meeting with management teams from the other vanguard institutions, the central project management teams, and Ex Libris. It was at these meetings that questions from the group sessions could potentially be asked. When the data sets from the three vanguard schools were finally loaded into the test environment, it was time to accomplish the phase 1 goal of replicating workflows. Select staff members were chosen to attempt to recreate their workflows within the new system and to document their progress step by step as they succeeded in replicating their workflows. After a draft workflow was created, it was then passed along to another staff member for testing to ensure that the results could be replicated. Once the workflow was validated, it was placed on the consortial website that acted as the central documentation repository for all member libraries (figure 13.1). Internally, workflows were shared with management and stored on Google Drive. This process was the prototype for the workflow creation and documentation procedures that would later be refined after the migration to Alma.

Phase 2: Post-Migration Documentation and Training

After GSU's go-live date for Alma, things did not go as planned for CRS. There were numerous factors that led to chaos in workflow processes and to mass disorganization. The first contributing factor was that in the months leading up to the go-live date, a cataloging freeze was put in place to ensure that people were not creating records after Ex Libris had pulled the data that would form the database for Alma. This created a backlog of purchased content that could not be cataloged until the new LMS went live. Secondly, there was no way during the pre-migration period to test any acquisitions functions that mimic real-world situations. Lastly, pre-migration documentation mostly fell to the

Workflow Title:
Adding Holding Records to Existing Bibliographic Records for Added Copies

Date: 02/10/2017

CRS Member: GASouth

Task Description: This workflow begins after a bibliographic record for physical resources has been added to Alma.

ALMA Menu Path: Alma Repository search

Area of Focus: Resource Management (Inventory)

Steps in the Process

Step 1: Perform a repository search for a record for the resource.

Step 2: Verify that the record is a match for the resource, based on the results list data.

Step 3: Click on Holdings from the Results list.

Step 4: Click on Add New Holdings.

Step 5: Begin editing the form. Select the Library from the drop-down menu.

Step 6: Select the Location in the library from the drop-down menu.

Step 7: Update the Call Number and Call Number type. Place the cursor in the Call Number field.

Step 8: Select Edit/Enhance the Record.

Step 9: Select Marc21 Holding Normalize from BIB on the drop-down menu and click OK.

Step 10: Place the cursor in the Copy Number field and enter the number only.

FIGURE 13.1
Early workflow documentation created during pre-migration

wayside in the immediate period after going live because the instructions hardly mirrored what had been practiced in the test environment and did not prove very helpful in real-world workflow tasks. This was because cataloging workflows, and acquisitions workflows that were not testable on the vanguard sandbox, were inextricably linked together.

Staff had to experiment with the new LMS and adjust the workflows that had been created during the vanguard testing period. Fortunately, the backlog of acquisitions materials, both print and electronic, turned out to be a blessing in disguise. These materials allowed CRS to refine the workflows created during the testing period. While processing these materials, mistakes had been made, but these served as powerful lessons of what staff could and could not do in Alma. After the initial rush of trying to catch up with the backlogged items and performing the first fiscal close in the system, it was time to get organized. The best way to do this was to go back to the group sessions from the pre-migration period in order to fix workflows and map how the work was now interconnected. The documentation process was also revamped as staff moved forward with creating and modifying the existing documentation.

Over multiple sessions, CRS staff, mostly those from Cataloging and Metadata and Continuing Resources, began the process of truly understanding how to work in the new system. The first step was to create a process-mapping diagram that highlighted how material traveled from person to person, and what needed to be done before it could be passed off to the next step in the workflow. This allowed each staff member to know what both they and their coworkers were responsible for within the process. Then began the process of working on the actual workflows themselves. By utilizing new and backlogged materials, staff went through individual workflows step by step. Each staff member, sitting at a conference table, moved through the system to complete the workflow. Since there were technically multiple ways to potentially achieve these workflows, staff were encouraged to consistently follow the same documented steps so as not to cause unintended consequences, and thus make it hard to diagnose where a problem had arisen within the overall process.

Next, staff were briefed on how the creation and documentation of workflows would go in the future. When staff discovered a new workflow, or a change in an existing workflow, they documented it. They then passed the new or edited workflow off to either management or another staff member to go through the workflow and verify that the results could be replicated. In order to standardize documentation, a workflow template was created. The template ensured that naming structure and workflow numbering remained consistent. There was also a place for the creator of the workflow to date and initial when they had finished. The creator passed off the workflow to a staff member who then tested the workflow again. After validating the workflow, the staff member marked that they were finished by initialing and dating the workflow in the appropriate place (figure 13.2). This system allowed both management and staff members to know who had touched a workflow last and when it had been tested and verified. Staff were also told to keep their instructions simple but detailed. This allowed others to step in and complete a staff member's step in the process if they were out, and it allowed a newly hired staff member to jump right into their role with the assistance of the preestablished workflows. The documentation was added to the newly revamped Collection and Resource Services manual, which was hosted on LibGuides. The former wiki, which housed the previous library system workflows, was now outdated, and was being shut down. Data from the old wiki was exported and sorted through by management to determine if anything needed to be migrated to the new wiki.

After getting workflows organized, revamping workflow documentation, creating a new centralized location for that documentation, and using collaborative group sessions to train staff, CRS entered a period of stability. Troubleshooting any issues that arose in the workflows or overall process was delegated to a member of management. Solutions for the issues that had been fixed were documented and then reviewed by the department head. A group session was scheduled to go over any changes in existing workflows and to allow staff members to ask questions. Anything that didn't require a group session was sent out in an e-mail or discussed at either the monthly CRS departmental meeting or the intersectional unit meetings. The overall process began to smooth itself out and enabled the department to function like a well-oiled machine. Everything was in place before the department had to embark on another major system-wide change.

Phase 3: Merger

There was an assumption that going live with a new LMS, and finally getting workflows and the overall process down, would allow for some downtime to get comfortable working within the system. However, that is not how things turned out. The University System of Georgia's Board of Regents voted, and it was announced that Georgia Southern University would merge with Armstrong State University to become one entity. This meant that every department had to work with their counterparts at the other university to ensure that a structure was in place before the schools' merger became official. For the library, it also meant that both instances of Alma had to be merged into one database. There also was a need for a reconciliation of workflows and an analysis of how the two teams would work together. Collection and Resource

Workflow: Adding Titles to a Collection from an Archived Backup

(rev 03/06/19, DDL; val MM/DD/YY, BBB)

This workflow describes the process needed to add titles to a collection from an archived collection backup file.

1. Log in to Alma.
2. Hover over "Admin" in the top toolbar.
3. Below "Manage Jobs and Sets," click "Manage Sets."
4. On the "Manage Sets" screen, click the "Add Set" button, and select "Itemized."
5. In the "Set Name" field, type the title of the collection.
6. Below "Add Contents from File to Set," click the Open Folder icon.
7. Navigate to the R Drive Archive folder.
8. Select the latest archived backup.
9. Click Open.
10. On the Set Details page, click "Save" in the top right-hand corner.
11. Hover over "Resources" in the top toolbar.
12. Below "Manage Inventory," click "Manage Collections."
13. Click the hyper-linked title of the collection that needs to be backed up. The hyperlinks will be in the "Collection Name" column.
14. On the "Collection Resource Editor" screen, click the "Add Titles from Set" button, located to the right of the "Add Title" button.
15. In the short search bar, with Name next to it, search for the title of the set you created.
16. Click the radio button next to the appropriate set once it has been found.
17. Click "Add Set Titles" in the top right-hand corner.
18. When prompted, click "Confirm."
19. A job will be run to add the titles to the collection from the set, and an email will be sent when the job is finished.

FIGURE 13.2
Updated workflow documentation with revision and validation dates and initials

Services wanted to accomplish three goals before the merger occurred. First, material types and circulation policies needed to be fixed and documented, and the staff trained on how to use them going forward. Second, there needed to be meetings with the technical services counterpart at Armstrong State University to develop a plan outlining how the two groups would function together moving forward. Lastly, the staff at both institutions needed to get to know each other and learn how each department functioned.

The material types and circulation policies cleanup was primarily handled by management, and by staff with a deep understanding of the technical services history of the institution. The group session method was employed to manage this cleanup, and multiple sessions were scheduled weekly to make the deadline date. As records were cleaned up, the group documented the changes to material types and circulation policies in a chart so that staff could have an evolving resource to consult. Collection and Resource Services management, and their counterparts from Armstrong State University, met and solicited feedback from staff as they moved forward with creating recommendations for how the merged department would work in the future. As a way for staff to get to know both each other and the ins-and-outs of how each department worked, both departments hosted each other at their libraries and participated in group activities. By the summer of 2018, the Alma environments of Georgia Southern University and Armstrong State University had been merged. Overall, the merger, from a technical services point of view, went well and allowed us to move forward with only minimal disruption to established workflows and the process.

LESSONS LEARNED

The migration from Voyager to Alma, while challenging at times, was a great learning experience and there were several key takeaways. First, it is important to document everything. Documentation is key to making sure there is a record for everything that must be done, to avoid repeating mistakes that were made in the past. It will also prevent personnel silos where large amounts of system and institutional knowledge will be lost with the departure of a single person. Second, it helps to be flexible. At any point there could be an unforeseen event that forces a deviation from the established plan. It is impossible to be ready for everything, so a healthy amount of flexibility will allow everyone to roll with the punches and get back on track. This leads to the next point: being willing to experiment and troubleshoot. In a system like Alma, where there are multiple paths to achieving the same outcomes, it can be beneficial to take the path not yet traveled. Experimentation can help us find more efficient ways to complete processes. Experimenting could also lead to the discovery of solutions to problems that were previously roadblocks in the workflow process. Eliminating those roadblocks increases efficiency, and the solution should be documented in case it happens again in the future. While experimenting has potential upsides, there are also potentially detrimental downsides. Experimentation could cause unforeseen consequences that disrupt not only one person's work, but the work of their colleagues as well. The experimentation and troubleshooting process should be handled by a select few to minimize potential disruptions and maximize the potential to find solutions and increase workflow efficiency.

The final two takeaways, patience and reassurance, go hand in hand. When going through a migration process, it is imperative to be patient and not get frustrated. Frustration spreads and can lead to an unproductive work environment that leads to mistakes being made in multiple places and multiple workflows. It is hard to learn a new system as a team when different people learn at different paces. But with patience, it will all come together, and everyone will eventually get on the same page. This is where reassurance comes into play. Staff need reassurance that everything is going to be okay, that their mistakes are not the end of the world, and most importantly, that everyone is in this together.

CONCLUSION

Collection and Resource Services took an internally new approach to staff training and how those processes and workflows were documented, which helped them achieve their primary training goals for staff. The staff now knew where their work fell within the new workflow chain and were encouraged, and empowered, to voice their concerns and provide input into the overall workflow. The staff also developed new skills through cross-training and could now accurately and easily document the work that they did daily. These new skills and the reorganization of the workflow process were essential in easing the transition to the merged environment with Armstrong State University, and enabled their staff to easily catch up and fit into the workflow process.

About the Editors and Contributors

Marlee Dorn Givens has been librarian for modern languages and a library learning consultant at the Georgia Tech Library since 2017, and liaison to the School of Psychology there since 2018. In this position she works with faculty in the schools of Modern Languages and Psychology to support their teaching and scholarship, provides classroom and online instruction, and facilitates learning for library employees. Marlee also holds two certificates in learning design from the Association for Talent Development.

Sofia Slutskaya is the head of resource description at Emory University's Woodruff Library. Over the years, Sofia has held a variety of positions in both public and technical services. Her research interests include staff training, cataloging print and electronic materials, e-resource management, and e-book acquisitions.

• • •

Beth Ashmore is the associate head of acquisitions and discovery, serials, at North Carolina State University Libraries. Her research interests include negotiation, troubleshooting metadata and electronic resources issues, and accessibility policy in libraries. She is the coauthor of *The Librarian's Guide to Negotiation.*

Juliya Borie is a cataloging librarian at the University of Toronto Libraries. She is responsible for serials metadata and French-language collections. Juliya finds inspiration in a collaborative, holistic approach to developing cataloging skills in staff and sharing resources and expertise. She coordinated RDA training at UTL, and was a language instructor before becoming a librarian. Her research interests include serials resource discovery, critical approaches to knowledge organization, and multilingual collections and services.

Tammie Busch is the catalog and metadata librarian and cataloging supervisor at Southern Illinois University Edwardsville. Tammie has over twenty years of experience working in public, school, and academic libraries. She received her MLS from the University of Missouri and an MA in history from Lincoln University in Jefferson City, Missouri.

May Chan is the head of metadata services at the University of Toronto Libraries. Having taught cataloging in a variety of settings, May is passionate about seeing a wide range of library folk empowered with technical skills to navigate the future. Her seventeen years of experience in public libraries have made her value service excellence and collaboration. Part of May's approach to leading change is to look for a critical mass of collaborators, embrace the diversity of roles they bring into an ecosystem, and develop them according to their strengths and interests.

Maria Collins is the head of acquisitions and discovery at North Carolina State University Libraries and has served in various capacities at NC State since 2005. She has over twenty years of library management experience. She is the former editor-in-chief of *Serials Review*, and has published in the areas of electronic resources management, open access, and workflows.

Jennifer R. Culley is the lead acquisitions librarian at the University of Nevada, Las Vegas. She received her MLIS degree from the University of Alabama. She has managed acquisitions units for the last nine years and has been at the University of Nevada, Las Vegas, since 2019.

Leslie A. Engelson is the metadata librarian at Murray State University. In her roles as a technical services librarian and a metadata librarian, Leslie has trained and supervised numerous staff and dozens of student workers. She seeks to incorporate tools and techniques that make the training process more efficient and effective, and she gets great satisfaction when a staff member or student worker is able to work independently and confidently.

Rachel K. Fischer is a member services librarian for technical services at Cooperative Computer Services. She has more than eight years of experience working in the field of technical services and has published articles in *Public Library Quarterly, Library Hi Tech,* and *Reference & User Services Quarterly,* as well as a book chapter. She has an MLIS degree from Dominican University and an MSM degree from Minot State University.

Marlee Graser was the metadata librarian and interim supervisor of digital initiatives and technology at Southern Illinois University Edwardsville from 2017 to 2020 before assuming her current role there as discovery and technology librarian in 2020. She also served as the interim supervisor of technical services at the university in 2018–19.

Hyun Chu Kim is the director of technical services at Kennesaw State University. She is responsible for leading the Technical Services unit, which encompasses the library's metadata and discovery and acquisitions subunits.

Daricus Larry is the systems and metadata librarian at the University of Arizona Libraries. His primaries duties include being the product lead for the LSP, Alma, coordination of the Systems Admin Group, development for Primo, cataloging, and metadata management.

Mai Lu is the head of public services at the University of Toronto Mississauga Library. Mai worked in public libraries for over fifteen years before transitioning to academic libraries. She holds a MISt degree from the University of Toronto and a master's degree in public policy, administration, and law from York University.

Kristen J. Nyitray is the director of Special Collections and University Archives and is the university archivist at Stony Brook University.

Jharina Pascual is the electronic resources acquisitions librarian at the University of California Irvine. Her areas of interest include information literacy, metadata, and electronic resource management. She received her undergraduate degree at Scripps College and her library science degree at the University of Michigan.

Dana Reijerkerk is the knowledge management and digital assets librarian at Stony Brook University.

Laura Sill is head of acquisitions at the University of Chicago Library and has held various management and leadership roles within technical services and library systems throughout her career. She believes that technical services staff have an adaptable skill set that positions them well for the broadening expectations within the field. During her 2020–2022 tenure as program director for metadata services at the Hesburgh Libraries at the University of Notre Dame, she focused on developing a community of practice to support metadata strategy as a means for promoting organization-wide learning between creators and consumers of resource metadata.

Xiaoyan Song is the electronic resources librarian, monographs, at North Carolina State University Libraries. She has many years of experience in e-resources management and is interested in evolving technical services with technology.

Elisa Sze is a metadata librarian at the University of Toronto Libraries. Elisa has a long-standing interest in how information professionals learn new skills, having trained staff, designed workshops, and supported and taught cataloging courses at the University of Toronto's Faculty of Information for over a decade. Her research interests are in planning around technical services and Canadian library history. Elisa's previous experience as a collections librarian and cataloging instructor at the university's Faculty of Information give her insight into the many training opportunities she regularly leads and supports.

Ariel Turner currently serves as associate dean for collections and discovery at Clemson University. She formerly served as the chair of the Department of Library Resources at Kennesaw State University, which encompasses the library's Technical Services, Collection Development, and Systems Units.

Polina Vendrova is a metadata creation specialist at the University of Toronto Libraries. She is a former elementary schoolteacher and is motivated to use her teaching skills to promote collegiality, cooperation, and knowledge-sharing within the department. Her experience in leading and supporting training gives her the insight and opportunity to observe other staff members' work processes and learn best practices from them. She continues to seek out opportunities to champion closer and more productive relationships in the workplace.

John White is currently the Gumberg Library's Simon Silverman Phenome-
nology Center Scholar-in-Residence. His research interests include phe-
nomenological influences on management theories and their application in
libraries.

Kristy White is currently the acquisitions librarian and a faculty member at
Duquesne University. Her primary research interests are organizational
and management theories in libraries, workflow management, contract
negotiations, and data privacy and analysis.

Lynn Whittenberger is the associate head of acquisitions and discovery, monographs, at North Carolina State University Libraries. She manages a staff
of seven licensing, acquiring, and cataloging monographic resources in all
formats, and database maintenance activities in the ILS, including batch-
loading MARC records. Lynn serves as a member of the ALA's CORE continuing education team.

Index